Cobblestones, Conversations, AND *Corks*

Cobblestones, Conversations, AND *Corks*

A SON'S DISCOVERY OF HIS ITALIAN HERITAGE

Giovanni Ruscitti

RADIUS BOOK GROUP
New York

Radius Book Group
A Division of Diversion Publishing Corp.
New York, NY
www.RadiusBookGroup.com

For more information, email info@radiusbookgroup.com.

First edition: August 2022
Hardcover ISBN: 978-1-63576-817-6
Paperback ISBN: 978-1-63576-796-4
eBook ISBN: 978-1-63576-819-0

Manufactured in the United States of America

1 3 5 7 9 10 8 6 4 2

Cover design by Jen Huppert Design
Interior design by Neuwirth & Associates, Inc.

To My Father

Author's Note

This book is a work of nonfiction. The conversations, memories, stories, and events are real. The historical events depicted in this book are from memories from my family and are not intended to be statements of fact. In some cases, I have changed names and identifying information to protect the privacy of others.

Table of Contents

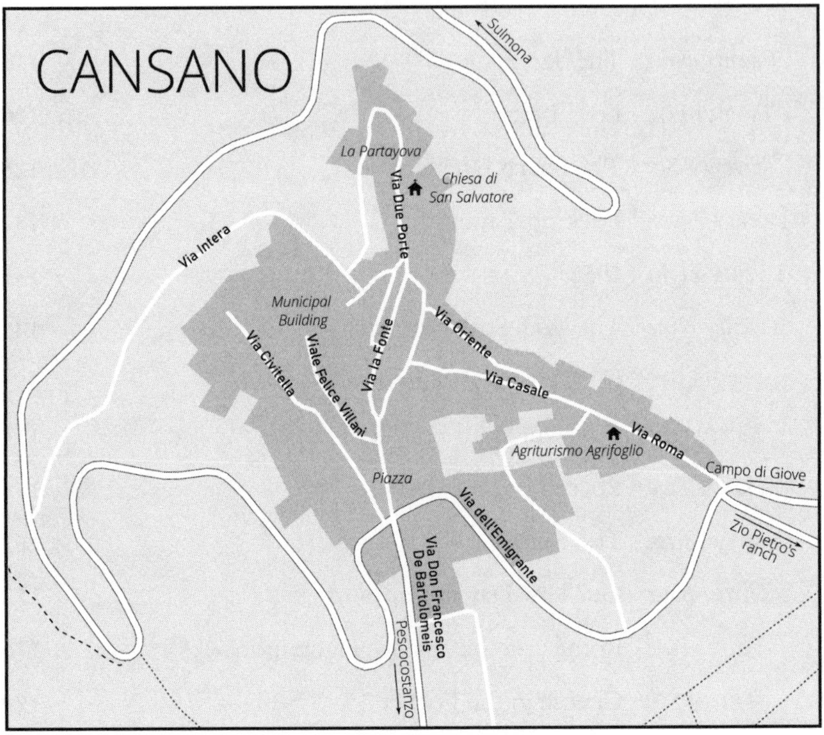
CANSANO
Sulmona
La Partayova
Chiesa di San Salvatore
Via Due Porte
Via Intera
Municipal Building
Via Oriente
Via Civitella
Viale Felice Villani
Via la Fonte
Via Casale
Via Roma
Agriturismo Agrifoglio
Campo di Giove
Zio Pietro's ranch
Piazza
Via dell'Emigrante
Via Don Francesco De Bartolomeis
Pescocostanzo

MARCHE
Milan
Vomano
Teramo
Adriatic
Sea
Gran Sasso d'Italia
Abruzzean Apennines
Pescara
L'Aquila
Chieti
Pescara
LAZIO
ABRUZZO
Popoli
Sangro
Maiella Mts.
Sulmona
Pacentro
Campo di Giove
Cansano
Rome
Pescocostanzo
MOLISE

CHAPTER ONE

The Road

As we drive up the two-lane road to Cansano in central Italy in June 2013, my heart races with anticipation and trepidation. Here I was at forty-six years old, *and I had never been here before*. My entire family, dating back many generations, was from this little town. I was a first-generation Italian American; my name was very ethnic; my first language was Italian; and, in many ways, I completely defined myself as being Italian. I was a bit resentful that my parents had never brought me here as a child. Though my three sisters had all been here, I was the only son and, even as a child, I was expected to stay back home and help maintain things there or, later, run the family business. But now, finally, here I was, driving up this road to Cansano with my wife Aggie, two of our three children, my parents, and my father's oldest brother Pietro, who still lived in Cansano.

The chauffeured van is quiet, its passengers tired from the long journey from Denver, a journey that included a layover in Charlotte, an eight-hour flight to Rome, and a two-hour drive toward the Adriatic Sea. As we continue on the winding road that cuts through the Maiella mountains, I am overcome with a strange sense of familiarity. When I was a child, my parents and grandparents regaled me with stories about this very valley and the life it brought my ancestors, stories about struggles and the simplicity of a peasant life. If my dad told me a story once, he told me the same story one hundred times; these stories were ingrained in me.

"Guarda la bellezza," my dad says, looking up the tree-lined road with mountains shooting up on both sides. "Look at the beauty."

As we drive past the entrance to Pacentro, an ancient town with a magnificent medieval castle that we would later visit, I briefly see Cansano in the distance, perched on top of a hillside—a cluster of small off-white buildings with pinkish roofs. Every love affair starts somewhere, and my love affair with my heritage and my family's story started with this view.

"Appeso su di un colle invisibile," wrote Nicolina D'Orazio Di Tunno about the view in her book, *La Pittoresca Terra di Cansano*. Translated, that means: "hanging on an invisible hill."

This is where I was from, yet I wasn't. Can you be from a place you have never experienced or touched? But—and without really having appreciated and understood it—I had been shaped by my town of origin, especially its determined and ambitious men, overcome with a longing to really know my own land. I was finally here and, as we drove up the road, I felt a calmness that would grow the longer I was here. In the years to come, I visited here often and became close to family that remained here, especially Zio (Uncle) Pietro. I walked the tiny streets with names like *Via Casale, Via Oriente, Via Intera, Via Civitella, Via Due Porte*, and *Via Umberto I* to discover where I was from, and I grew to appreciate my ancestors and what made them who they were, especially my father.

And I learned more about who I am.

CHAPTER TWO

Chopping Wood and the Market

Cansano disappears, and I am entranced by the olive groves and vines on the outskirts of Pacentro as we begin our gradual climb up the winding road to our destination. I think about the many stories I had heard about Cansano, this V-shaped valley, and the Abruzzo region of Italy that the olive groves and vines sit in. In the 1930s and 1940s, this winding tree-lined road was a trail, traversed mostly by foot, mule, and donkey. A creek, now dry, once flowed through the valley from Cansano to Pacentro, and was a source of life for the people of Cansano, called *Cansanesi*. In the 1930s, the valley was rich in timber, fruit and nut trees, and limestone, and was dotted with tiny farms where Cansanesi would plant their crops and take their few livestock to pasture. The timber was used as currency in Sulmona, a town of about 25,000 people located in *Valle Peligna*, a plateau once occupied by a lake in prehistoric times. Just above sea level, the people of Sulmona relied on the mountain peasants for firewood in the 1800s and 1900s.

As we drive, my dad starts telling a story I had heard before and would hear again.

"I was young. I had a mule and a donkey. They sent me to pick up the wood. The older people, they cut the wood, four meters long, one meter high. And like anybody, a good woodcutter, they make one or two good cords a day—no chainsaws. I was just a little kid at the time. My mom and my dad, they send me with the mule and the donkey, and

I load the wood in the high country where all those older people cut it and get paid for it. One time, I get to a place we stored the wood and there is quite a bit of snow on the ground. It was winter and so cold my hands were frozen. I load up the mule and the donkey and it gets to the point where I can't do it no more."

He pauses, studying the mountain, perhaps recalling the exact location where it occurred.

He continues. "The forest guy comes up. He knows my dad and says, 'Emiliano, are you doing OK? Here, let me help you. I'll help finish the load and get you on the road back home.' And he did that, and I will never forget that. Otherwise, I would have been in a lot of trouble; I had no gloves, I was a little kid."

Like many of the towns in the Abruzzo region of central Italy, Sulmona's story is deep and rich, with connections to the Roman, Medieval, and Renaissance periods. It was devastated by an earthquake—a common experience in this region of Italy—in 1706, destroying much of the medieval city. An aqueduct, built in the 1200s under Holy Roman Emperor Frederick II, survived. Years later, I would walk with my parents, who were holding hands, under its lancet arches made with hewn stone as we entered Piazza Garibaldi to visit the Wednesday market.

The piazza and market in Sulmona were an integral part of our past and shaped my father and our family's future. My father loved the market. He loved to barter and to think he had outsmarted the vendor to get the "deal." I recall many times when I was a child and walking with my dad into a store like Sears or Kmart to buy something we needed.

He would tell a clerk—usually a young person making minimum wage and with zero authority to do anything other than stock the shelves—something like, "This table saw is not worth two hundred dollars. I will give you fifty."

I would watch in embarrassment as the clerk responded, "Uh, the price is two hundred."

"Dad, you can't do that!" I would say. "This is Kmart. You can't negotiate prices!"

"Sonza bitches," he would say walking out of the store. "They are stealing from people."

"And don't be afraid to ask for a better price," he often added. "Why can't you ask for a better price?"

Years later, I would see him in action at the Sulmona markets and finally understand. And in the end, it was the last thing he wanted to experience in Vail, Colorado.

My father, like my mother and my grandparents, often sold the wood he had hand cut and hauled through the valley to the piazza in Sulmona for a few lira to help the family. A load of wood earned them the equivalent of a few dollars, and the family then bought the things they could not grow or make themselves. After the transaction, my dad and his friends would stop and eat a panini, which they would enjoy with a glass of wine. He was twelve years old. After lunch, they filled their flasks with water from a fountain on the northern end of the piazza and then headed back to Cansano on their twelve-kilometer hike with the goods and any remaining profits from their sale. This is one of the many stories my father had told me over the years. When I first heard them, the stories had no context; I heard them so many times I, regrettably, stopped listening. In later years, he described the trips to my son, Dante, as follows:

> We walked three, four, five miles sometimes to get to places. You cut the wood with a hatchet. I remember with my dad or my friends, we went to the market, and sold wood. Sometimes we would stop to have a sandwich, bread, mortadella, get a bottle of wine. The kids—I was just ten, eleven, twelve—would have a little bit. Water was free too. You didn't pay for water those days. The poor people, they work very hard, they want the wine—but it wasn't like the bottles over here. At the market, you look at the animals and goods, find the owner, and say, "How much you want?" You negotiate the price.

"We had nothing after the war," my dad often told me in my childhood. "Poor is not the right word."

World War II hit the Abruzzo region of Italy very hard. Two factors of nature conspired to bring on this hardship: The central location—one hundred miles east of Rome and forty-six miles from the Adriatic Sea—made it a strategic corridor for both the Nazis and Allied forces, and the mountainous surroundings and hillside towns like Cansano with their centuries-old fortified walls provided great shelter for the troops. And unlike other European countries, Italy experienced the horrors of war from both sides: first from the Nazis when they occupied the region in late 1943 and enslaved the locals to help them with the war effort and then from bombings from Allied forces trying to drive the Nazis north and Italy, and its fascist leader Benito Mussolini, to capitulate. These horrors culminated in 1944 with the long and deadly battle of Sangro River, a river to the southeast of Cansano, when whole villages and towns were destroyed by Nazi and American bombings. Even if towns survived, as Cansano did, the damage was deep and incomprehensible. My father often talked about the war and how everyone, regardless of their country, behaved in a regrettable fashion, forgetting human decency in the name of fighting for a country.

"It was horror," he told me. "*Miseria.*" Misery.

As we continue our drive to Cansano, I think about the war and his stories. The mountains on each side of the valley are steep, dense with trees and filled with rocky cliffs. How did they make those trips on foot or mule with hundreds of pounds of wood, I wonder? And then hike back home? I watch my father and he is quiet, lost in thought, undoubtedly remembering his past.

CHAPTER THREE

The Wine Cellar

Back home in 2013, my life is good. Indeed, I am blessed. Aggie and I married young, raised each other, and were raising three children and building our lives, together. Dante was entering his junior year in college, Donato was entering his senior year in high school, and Izabella was entering her freshman year in high school. And while they would each go through the challenges of becoming young adults in the years to come (testing our parental will and patience along the way), they were good people and were on their way to becoming productive, thoughtful, and kind contributors to society. My law practice was growing; a few years later, I would become managing partner of our firm and watch my legal and arbitration practice grow exponentially, working with great clients on matters of importance and significance. My firm, Berg Hill Greenleaf Ruscitti LLP, which I cofounded in 2001 with George Berg, David Hill, and Rick Greenleaf, had already become the largest firm in Boulder, and we would soon expand with offices in Denver, Cheyenne, San Diego, and Irvine. Daily life consumed us, and I prioritized my young family and career over everything else. I talked to my parents every few days and saw them every few weeks. But they were retired and had a more active social life than I did. Their home had an open door policy for neighbors and friends, and my parents loved cooking for people. And, above all, my dad loved sharing his homemade wine and wisdom.

My father and I had, in many ways, a classic father-son relationship. In other ways, our relationship was not typical. I spent my weekends as a young boy helping him in the garage making furniture and picture frames for the house. He was an incredibly skilled carpenter, and I wondered when and how he learned the skill. A common lecture included his saying, "Don't be afraid. You can do anything." And he made everything in that garage, including beautifully crafted tables, cutting boards, and a headboard for my sister's waterbed.

On fall and winter weekends, I accompanied him to my maternal grandfather Panfilo's (Paul) wine cellar a few blocks from my house to make wine, prosciutto, and dried sausages. The cellar was underground and made from old red bricks and limestone rocks by my maternal great-grandfather Falco, who lived in the home right after World War II. Falco replicated the architecture he knew from Italy. Round hooks hung from the ceiling. Three wine barrels lined each side of the cellar, some full, some empty, and the old wine press with a worn red handle was at the end of the cellar. A few transfer barrels used in the wine-making process filled the open spaces of the cellar, and six to eight prosciuttos hung from the arched ceiling of the cellar.

The smell from that cellar was unforgettable and comforting: wet stone, dark red fruit, salt and pepper, damp and wet earth, old corks, nuts, cobwebs, old wood, and musk. Each year, the old Cansanesi living in the Denver area ordered pallets of zinfandel, muscat, and chardonnay grapes from California for delivery in October. Each family would take the number of boxes of grapes they needed to make wine for their families. Buying wine in a store or restaurant was unheard of and almost sacrilegious.

"That stuff is junk," my dad would say. "Who knows what they put in there? Sugar, water, chemicals. Junk!"

Later in life, when I was in my forties and he in his seventies, I was fortunate to take him and my mom to many restaurants and on many trips where we drank great wines. And he soon changed his mind. But it was always quickly followed with, "Not bad. But my wine is better. We should sell it. You get rich."

After the grapes arrived, we spent weeks making wine, each night and weekend going to the cellar and carefully going through the process—first crushing and pressing using an old wine press imported from Italy, then fermenting in old oak barrels purchased from whiskey country, followed by transferring the wine into other barrels for aging, and finally bottling the wine from the year before.

Regardless of the grape my father used, his wine was a deep burgundy color and, sometimes, effervescent. And it was strong. The whiskey barrels gave the wine a certain aroma and taste unlike any wine I tasted as an adult. The wine wasn't bad, but it wasn't good either. I always mixed a little Sprite or 7 Up in the wine.

The only wine the old Cansanesi bought was Carlo Rossi Paisano or Carlo Rossi Chianti, jug wines made by the E&J Gallo Winery in California. In the 1970s, it cost two to three dollars per jug. Not the best wine for sure. But the Cansanesi, like every other Italian immigrant I knew in Denver, bottled their wine in these old jugs. Using those bottles seemed like a source of pride, almost as a symbol that they had arrived and *made it*. But they needed more bottles and since buying new bottles was out of the question—"Why would you do that?" my father would ask—my dad took me on weekends to restaurants in Longmont, a city twelve miles away from our hometown of Frederick, not to eat but to collect bottles and corks.

My dad thought going to restaurants was a waste. "For the amount you would spend one night, you can buy enough pasta or rice to feed a family of six for a week," he would often counsel.

We asked restaurants if they had wine bottles and corks left over from wine consumed the night before. I was always slightly embarrassed and wondered what they thought of the crazy Italians asking for empty wine bottles and used corks.

"I will bring you some of my wine," my dad would tell the owner. "You will love it." And he always honored that promise. He would sit with the restaurant owner and drink the wine. In fact, promises were very important to him. "A good man always does what he says he is going to do," was another common adage.

We walked out of the restaurants with several cases of empty bottles. Many still sit in his garage today in 2022.

The smell of the wine grapes themselves, which are different from grapes you purchase in the market, is memorable. Even to this day, when shopping at a grocery store, I inexplicably stop by the grapes and pick up a cluster, hoping to get a smell from my past. Occasionally, the market sells muscat grapes, which I buy more for the aroma than to eat.

My father and grandfather each made his own wine in that same small, cramped cellar. From what I could tell, they used the same grapes and process. The only difference was the barrels they used—each owning his own.

"My wine is a little better," my grandfather said to my dad.

"*Ma, tu sei pazzo,*" my dad responded to his father-in-law.

"You are crazy." My grandpa chuckled.

Same conversation every year. In reality, the wines were about the same.

In addition to prosciutto, the cellar was also used to hang dried sausages that they made each December and January, as well as rounds of provolone and other Italian cheeses purchased in bulk from Italian markets in north Denver. As it turns out, the climate in Colorado was very similar to the climate in Cansano, so my father and grandfather were able to continue their old-world traditions.

Each October, they cut the prosciutto they'd made the prior December, and we would have a simple feast of my mom's or grandmother Nunziata's homemade crusty bread, prosciutto, dried sausages, cheese, a red wine vinegar salad with cucumbers and tomatoes, and wine. As a young boy, my grandfather and father would pour me a small glass of their wines.

"*Questo ti rendera un uomo,*" my grandpa Panfilo would tease. "This will make you a man."

The process of cutting the prosciutto from the year before was an event. This was a product of their days in Cansano where, in the 1930s and late 1940s, families of four, five, or six would count on two or three prosciuttos to last the whole year. The prosciutto would be cut only on holidays or special occasions, and every part of it would be used—the fatty trim used as cooking shortening and the bone used for soups. In my grandfather's cellar, my father and grandfather would carefully cut the prosciutto, hoping the dried meat had not gone bad. They would cut a thick piece and tear it into three pieces, one for each of us, and we would all taste it at the same time. A good prosciutto is bright pink in color and has a soft, sweet aroma of dried fruit, hazelnuts, and butter, which is countered by the smell of salt and pepper used to season the prosciutto. If the prosciutto was good, there was laughter, congratulations, and wine. If it went bad—meaning it didn't cure properly and turned rancid or acidic—the Italian cuss words would flow. As would the wine, a common denominator in the equation.

The food, wine, and smells from that old cellar were tantalizing, and my romance with food and wine was born.

Other fall weekends we hunted in the Colorado foothills, and my springs and summers were spent fishing with Dad and his brother, Luciano; my grandpa, Panfilo, and his brothers Rocco and Antonio; and their friends from Cansano. The family was always together. I didn't know any other life.

Some weekends we butchered goats and lamb for holiday meals or dinner with special guests visiting from out of town. In the '70s and '80s, we always seemed to have other Italian immigrants over for a special meal. "You have to learn how to do this," Dad said of the butchering process.

So, while other children in my town were playing, developing friendships, riding bikes, and learning American sports from their fathers, I was *always* with these old, Italian immigrant men, learning how to butcher a goat, make wine and dried meats, and work with wood. By the time I was a young teenager, I almost resented this way of growing up and wished I could just be *normal*. As I grew older—especially after this trip to Italy—I discovered that I was wrong.

CHAPTER FOUR

Pulling Weeds

Like many of his fellow Cansanesi, my father embraced a way of living and thinking marked by what he considered indelible truths, which was both good and bad for me. The good: he was fiercely proud, honest, a defender of what he believed and what he thought was right, industrious, innovative, loyal, magnanimous, and a provider. The bad: he was overly strict (especially with my sisters); a tough-love disciplinarian; distrustful of others; rigid; unwilling to suffer the fool, lazy person, or victim; quick-tempered; filled with stereotypical Italian machismo; and frugal. I, on the other hand, was into sports—playing football, basketball, and baseball and running track in high school. I loved to lift weights and work out. I loved the NFL and NBA. Dad loathed those activities, saying, "If you want to grow muscles, work with your hands. Build something." Or with respect to professional sports, "Look at those jokers! Are they worth all that money when the real men are working in farms or building something with their hands? They will never put food on your table."

Later in life, as an attorney, I occasionally represented—and therefore was paid by—parties involved in professional sports; Dad's words about sports not putting food on the table proved to be wrong.

My father had me pulling weeds by hand every summer when I was a young teenager. Many of my friends got to hang out while I was stuck in our backyard or in the quarter-acre lot to the side of the home Dad owned. It would take me days to pull weeds, and I did it every few weeks.

One summer when I was twelve or thirteen years old, Dad obtained a truckload of wood—free, of course—from a home that had just been torn down. The wood was full of nails and screws that my father had me pull out. Not with an electric tool, but by hand, with a hammer and screwdriver. He wanted to repurpose the wood or use it for firewood. It took weeks of hard labor in the hot sun.

"G, let's go ride bikes," my friends Jerry and Dino would say.

"I can't. I have to do work for my dad."

"Work?"

I hated having to do this and not being able to be with my friends. I just wanted to be normal.

All of this made for a love-hate relationship with my father when I was young and as I grew into a father myself. I emulated the good but didn't understand and eventually begrudged the bad. As a result, in my twenties and thirties, we didn't do much together.

In her book *A Year of Miracles*, Marianne Williamson writes, "I cannot know the deeper forces at work within anyone's heart. . . . It is not my job to monitor anyone's journey, to know what's right or wrong for others, or to try to control their behavior. My salvation lies in the deep acceptance of people exactly as they are."

I didn't appreciate this message until my forties and this 2013 trip to Cansano. People are who they are and, in many respects, are a product of their upbringing. The nature of self, identity, and who we truly are has been the subject of much intellectual, religious, and philosophical discussion. But we are a mixture of experiences, deeply engrained impressions of who we are (and are not) that form as children, socioeconomic backgrounds, genetics, ethnicity, education, jobs, history, family status, heritage, religion, thoughts, and imaginations.

My dad was a product of a difficult environment, which informed, if not dictated, his behavior. I didn't get this when I was younger.

But forgiveness is freedom, and by our 2013 trip to Cansano, Dad's edges had softened and much of the "bad" had dissolved, primarily after he survived a massive heart attack a decade earlier, and I was starting what would become a journey of self-growth and identity. This inaugural trip to Cansano—together with life coaching from my wife Aggie, a healthier lifestyle, and, later, spirituality and meditation—was part of the beginning of that process.

Most people don't know themselves, and it often takes some tragedy or revelation for people to discover their identities. I was about to see Dad for who he was.

CHAPTER FIVE

The Piazza

As the two-lane road cuts a path through the densely wooded valley, I get occasional glimpses of Cansano unfolding in front of me and to my left. Soon the town appears, as if out of nowhere, overtaking the valley leading back to Sulmona. Like hundreds of towns in Abruzzo, Cansano was originally fortified with thick walls protecting its interior and is perched on the mountainside to avoid the many dangers of primitive life—namely gangsters and thieves.

The stone buildings with red tiled roofs look much older than I imagined. There are two main entrances into town—one from the north, from the town of Sulmona, which is where we came from, and one from the south facing toward Pescocostanzo, another ancient town about twenty minutes away. The limited access left Cansano isolated for centuries, creating a self-sufficient and industrious, yet solitary, society.

We continue our slow climb, and the town plays peekaboo—appearing and disappearing and then appearing again as the wooded landscape flashes by our car window.

The recorded history of Cansano dates back to at least the 1100s. Relying on early descriptions of the town from writings from the archives of Pope Clement III (the head of the Catholic Church in the late 1100s), early writers such as Filippo Cirelli described the town in *The Kingdom of the Two Sicilies* as follows: "Between the Morrones and first Apennines, where a passage from Pescocostanzo to the plain of Sulmona was opened, sits the picturesque village of Cansano, its houses built with stones and lime, all aimed at noon."

This is the same sight I see on this June 2013 morning.

Just outside of town, a few kilometers away, is the archaeological site of Ocriticum. "Juwaa," my dad calls out my nickname that only he, my mom, and the old Cansanesi used. "Up the mountain and in an opening is an old ancient town they just discovered," he says, pointing to the right. "We need to see it." We ended up not having time this trip, but I visited the area with my dad the following year and, in 2017, I visited the site again with an old historian from Cansano, who told me its story: Ocriticum was a town that was home to a few hundred residents over 2,500 years ago. According to early records, the site included a settlement, a cemetery, and a sanctuary, which was occupied between the end of the fourth century BC and midway through the second century AD. An earthquake in the second century AD likely damaged many of the stone structures, which initiated gradual abandonment of the entire area right up until the sixth century. Sometime thereafter the town of Cansano emerged.

Since Ocriticum's discovery in 1992, archeologists at the site have discovered three buildings on two levels. On the upper level are two major temples, both situated within enclosed areas: one from the fourth century BC dedicated to Hercules and one from the first century AD dedicated to Jupiter. On the lower level within a small enclosure is a smaller temple from the second century BC, which is dedicated to the goddesses Ceres and Venus.

After another turn, Cansano emerges again briefly through the emerald-green landscape. I think again about the stories my family passed down to me about this land, including the many stories of struggle, poverty, despair, and suffering that my family endured during and after World War II. I think about my paternal grandfather Rocco, whom I never met. He served in the Abyssinian War in Ethiopia and then in Libya at the beginning of World War II, and I wonder how many times he walked this now-paved road. The thought disappears as I catch another view of Cansano through the dense wood.

We were all tired from the long trip from Denver, but I refused to acknowledge any sleepiness, too nervous about my ability to communicate with my uncle, cousins, and other relatives in Cansano. My parents were immigrants, my grandparents spoke little or no English, I grew up learning the Cansanesi Italian dialect as my first language, and I took three years of proper Italian in college to fulfill my language requirements, but I didn't speak Italian and was worried about being able to carry out daily conversations. The first language my sisters and I learned was the Italian dialect my parents spoke, and, as a result, we struggled with English in elementary school. Indeed, in order to avoid having to repeat first grade, I had to attend summer school between first and second grade. I was humiliated, and I vowed never to speak Italian again. And with the exception of talking to my grandparents and taking Italian in college, I didn't. So I didn't want to embarrass myself in front of my Zio Pietro and his sons Rocco and Panfilo, whom I had only met briefly when they separately visited the United States in the '80s and '90s. I had been studying some Italian CDs in my F-150 pickup truck on my way to work for months but didn't have confidence that I would be able to carry out daily conversations.

As we drive up the mountainous road toward Cansano, I think back a few weeks and about the Italian CD and smile. One early May morning about a month before our trip, I found myself waiting for my dad outside my garage. The air was cold. As I exhaled, the water vapor in my breath condensed into millions of tiny droplets of liquid water and a white fog lofted into the air. My dad and I were going fly-fishing before the Colorado spring runoff. My dad was more of a worm dragger, but I had been trying to get him into fly fishing for years. He also did not understand catch and release.

"Why catch the fish if we are just releasing them?"

"Dad, it improves native fish populations by allowing more fish to remain and reproduce in the ecosystem. This increases the numbers of fish and makes it better long-term."

"I don't like it. They should discount the license fee then."

A version of this conversation happened every time we fished.

He arrived on time, as always. I started my truck and the Italian CD was playing.

"What is this?"

"I have been studying Italian to get ready for the trip."

When the instructor on the CD says something in English, you are supposed to translate the phrase or sentence into Italian. After a few seconds, the instructor then translates the English into Italian.

"This is good," Dad said. "Listen to the beauty of the language. They speak proper Italian."

My dad translated the next English sentence into Italian, as if he were the student. He did this several times.

"Good job, Dad," I teased. "You are learning."

My concerns about being able to have conversations in Italian proved ill-founded, as I did fine, especially with each glass of wine I drank, which was a lot.

^ ^ ^ ^ ^

The road to Cansano curves to the left, exposing a soccer field on the right, and after a short distance, we make our final turn right. And there in front of us is the town.

Something is very different about this town, and I sense it immediately, even in the van. The stillness and calm is unlike anything I had experienced previously, and time appears to stand still. To our left is *Piazza XX Settembre*, the town center where all of the remaining shops are located. In its center is a monument of soldiers—a feature often found in Abruzzo towns—a tribute to the Cansanese men that lost their lives in World War I, World War II, and the Spanish War. In the coming days, I visited the piazza often and read the surnames of fallen soldiers listed on the monument. They were familiar—all family names I had known or heard but with which I had no real connection. The town appears to be decaying, but in the most noble of ways, and looks like it was forgotten by time.

Past the monument in the distance sits the old municipal building that served as the town government and school when the town was thriving.

"That is where we went to school," my mom says.

"Only until the fifth grade," my dad quickly responds.

"And then we had to work to help the family. Very few people went to school past the fifth grade."

A few old men sit outside the *Locanda Cansanese*, a small *vineria* in the piazza, sipping wine from short glasses and, by their animation and loud passionate voices, having a very serious debate. I wonder if they knew my grandfathers. The rest of the piazza is empty and the town is completely quiet.

I watch my mom and dad, seeing the memories of their childhood rush back to them. I had heard so many stories about this town and its people, the piazza, the municipal building, their teachers, and their struggles. But their stories were always told with reverence and wistful longing. Now, an air of melancholy surrounds them. Yet, they are proud, too. They are excited that Aggie, Donato, Izabella, and I are finally seeing their ancestral home. (Dante could not make the trip because of school.) My father takes a deep breath but says nothing. Over the next few years, this moment stuck with me, along with some of the stories Dad had recounted that I had either forgotten, not appreciated, or never understood in the first place. In the years to come, moments and stories eventually started to come together to have meaning. I wish I had had more time with him.

CHAPTER SIX

The Town

My father, Emiliano Palmiero Ruscitti, was born in Cansano on Palm Sunday on April 5, 1936, to Rocco Ruscitti and Filomena De Angelis Ruscitti. He had two older brothers named Armando and Pietro, a younger brother named Luciano, and a younger sister named Anna. My mother, Maria, was born three years later in Cansano to Panfilo DiGiallonardo and Nunziata D'Orazio DiGiallonardo. She was the oldest child and had three sisters named Liberta, Emily, and Angela, and a brother named Luciano. My parents' families, and all of their ancestors dating back to at least the 1500s, were from Cansano.

While lacking in many ways economically, Cansano was a thriving social community in 1936. Over two thousand people lived in a type of agri-urban environment that was prolific in Europe during the 1920s and 1930s. The town was rich in culture and tradition, and the community was sustained by the tiny family farms surrounding the town and the natural water sources. *Piazza XX Settembre* served as the community hub. Before the war, a *salumeria* (small market), a bar (Italians refer to a coffee shop as a bar), a beer-and-wine establishment appropriately named *Vino e Birra*, and a *tabacchi* (a tobacco shop), as well as a few tailor and shoemaker shops, dotted the piazza in the 1930s.

A railroad constructed in the late 1800s connected the town to neighboring mountain villages and bigger cities. My father often reminded me that life was simple, hard, centered around family, and not burdened by material possessions. The people were—by any objective standard—poor, and progress was slow, but people were happy. The men from Cansano, including my great-grandfather Cassiodoro Ruscitti, left for the United States to build a better life. My father often talked about his great-grandfather, who came to America in the early 1900s only to return to Cansano after declaring, "I left a civilized country and found the wild west that was uncivilized!" The grass was not greener.

The Ruscitti family lived in *La Partayova*, a tiny neighborhood in the oldest part of town that was on the northern side between *Due Porte*—two massive doors with thick walls erected on the ends of the town entrance to keep the "gangsters" out. The family home was on *Via Due Porte*, a steep stairway made of cobblestones harvested from the local mountains. In our second trip to Cansano in 2014, my father told me that each cobblestone along the passageway was matching, six inches deep and four inches wide, carefully cut by mallet and pick. One- and two-story homes made from local stone were closely packed along the *Via*. The architecture was the classic *Abruzzesi* style seen in most hilltop towns in the region. The walls were thick and made of stone and lime. The floors in some rooms were made of lime, some of hard dirt.

Some homes had a fireplace and one or two bedrooms that all of the family shared. Hooks hung from the cobblestone ceilings from which families cured prosciutto, dried sausages, and cheeses. The homes of the 1930s lacked plumbing; some in the new part of town had electricity. Most families kept their cattle, sheep, and horses in stables built below the houses. The body heat and manure from the animals helped keep the homes warm in winter.

In the 1920s and 1930s, families stayed close to each other, literally and figuratively. Most of the Ruscitti family lived along a small stretch of *Via Due Porte* and shared living areas. One family had an oven for making bread while another had a large table for sharing family meals. The cousins shared bedrooms—the original "sleepover." They shared their harvests and were mini social units.

My mom's family lived in the "new" part of town along *Via Roma* on the way to Campo di Giove, which is now a local ski town only two miles away. Her home overlooked the deep valley below the town and the high mountain on the other side of the valley, with a magnificent terrace extending over the sharp decline. The home and area hold many memories. In 1943, after the Nazis invaded and occupied the town, the Cansanesi escaped through the valley below my mom's home to hide out in the mountains and caves. When he was seventeen and she was fourteen, my father serenaded my mom from the area below her home. Many years later we stayed at my cousin Rocco's bed-and-breakfast across the street from my mom's childhood home and were able to see the terrace in person.

CHAPTER SEVEN

His First Wages

Seeing the piazza for the first time on this June 2013 afternoon, my mind briefly takes me to stories of my parents' childhood homes, and I am anxious to see *La Partayova,* the neighborhood where my dad grew up. I think back to what my parents created for us after their arrival from Italy. My first childhood home was not much different from theirs in Cansano. In December 1954, Mom's family emigrated from Cansano to Frederick, Colorado, to escape the deep poverty caused by World War II. Frederick became an unlikely sister town to Cansano, with many Cansanesi moving there for jobs. They developed a new language—what I call *Frederickesi*—a mixture of their Cansanesi dialect and rough English. The men, largely unskilled and uneducated, found work in the local coal mines. Many died from accidents in the mines or from black lung disease, including my paternal great-grandfather Pietro De Angelis, who died in a mine outside of Frederick in 1946, and my maternal grandfather Panfilo, who died in 1982 from lung cancer when I was fifteen years old. One by one, men came to the United States to look for work. Once they were settled with work, they sent back money and eventually moved their wives and children to the United States. They also helped other Italians immigrate to the US, as immigrants had to be "sponsored" by US citizens, who vouched for the immigrants and supported them and helped them find employment. My dad took this seriously, and he sponsored several Cansanesi and other Italians from small towns in their region, helping each get a job.

My mom and her family started their new lives in Colorado. She returned to Cansano in 1957 to marry my father. She came back to Colorado alone, however, as my father needed a work sponsor in the United States before he could move to America. The next year he reunited with my mom in Frederick.

When he arrived, he found many comforts from home. Frederick was filled with Cansanesi, and Italian was the language of the small, western American town. In fact, the first language my two older sisters and I learned was Italian, and we struggled with English in elementary school.

In the late 1960s and early 1970s Frederick was much like Cansano. Most of the Cansanesi immigrants butchered their own goats and sheep; made homemade wine, sausage, pasta, cheese, and prosciutto; and lived in tight family clusters. My father, with his fifth grade Italian education, took any job he could get, including construction, pouring and finishing cement, and working as a laborer on highway construction projects. He spoke no English and worked two to three jobs, making under $1.20 per hour to support his young family.

My sister Rina was born in 1960, and the family rented a small home across the street from Dad's grandmother Lucia De Angelis, who went by her middle name, Anastasia. The street was dotted with other Cansanesi—no less than eleven families lived in a three-block area near our home on Sixth Street—and they supported each other as they had in Italy.

When I was a child, every holiday was an event. By the mid-1970s, all of my mother's and father's siblings lived in Frederick, except for Zio Pietro, who stayed in Cansano because his wife did not want to leave her family. We rotated homes to celebrate Thanksgiving, Christmas Eve, Christmas Day, New Year's Eve, New Year's Day, and Easter. Before settling in for the multicourse meals around a large table of twenty to thirty people, with the children at the obligatory children's table, my dad and I would visit my parents' aunts, uncles, cousins, and godparents who also resided in Frederick. As we entered each home, we were greeted with hugs, kisses, and commands to "*bevi*" (drink) and "*mangia*" (eat) as they presented their own homemade wines, *pizzelle* (Italian anise-flavored cookies), *cioffe* (fried sweet doughnuts), prosciutto, dried sausages, and cheeses. My dad brought a bottle of wine, whiskey, or grappa as an offering to each home. We visited two to four families, including my great-uncle Antonio, my mom's uncle, who was a big fan of my father and, later, of me.

You could not say no to offerings of food or drink—that is one of the worst offenses and insults in our culture. And so, as my dad caught a small buzz from the wine and liquors, I had my fill of 7 Up, Sprite, Squirt, or the other favorite soda of the lady of the house. By the time I was twelve, I graduated to small amounts of wine mixed with 7 Up to wash down endless streams of Italian cookies. My father was charming, engaging, and an expert small talker, and I learned the art of conversation during these visits.

Emiliano was an entrepreneur and hard worker. "Don't pay rent, buy a home!" he would lecture his grandchildren. "You are making other people rich by renting." And in the early 1960s, on his sparse earnings, and even though he was sending money back to Cansano to help his parents and siblings, he purchased the home he was renting, for $2,400. An hourly wage of $1.14 in 1962 was roughly equivalent to $4.86 per hour in 1993 when I got my first lawyer job making $56,000 a year.

"*Auguri* (congratulations)," my father told me when I proudly told him about my first job.

"I made $35,000 total from 1959 to 1982. You have so many more opportunities than I did," he told me in his thick accent that had survived over thirty years in America.

"If I only had your opportunities. I would really be something," he said. He said this often.

By most standards, we were poor growing up. But I didn't know it, as we were not lacking. By the 1970s, my dad had expanded our home on Sixth Street in Frederick, adding a bathroom (it had only an outhouse in the 1960s), two bedrooms, a laundry room, and a large living room. He did it himself. "I am not hiring anyone to do anything I can do myself," he would say. "You can do anything."

And he did. In the '70s, Dad and his brother Luciano formed a construction company and built numerous new homes on weekends and after work. He tried starting such a company in the '60s with my grandpa Panfilo and his brothers Antonio, Felice, and Rocco, but they were older and not as confident.

"What do we know about construction? *Tu sei pazzo*," they said. "You are crazy."

"What do you mean," he responded. "We are working construction and making everyone else rich. If they can do it, why can't we?"

I heard this story dozens of times, even in my forties.

And when I was a boy, Dad often said, "Juwaa, don't be afraid of anything. You can do it."

A memory: I was a junior in high school and I was sitting in advanced calculus class. The class was small, maybe twelve students, and I had known all of them since elementary school. I was a good student and graduated third in my class. But the teacher, Mr. Grant, didn't like me. He didn't like athletes, and I was the starting quarterback on the football team and starting shooting guard on the basketball team, and I ran track and went to the state track meet. And I had always sensed that he didn't like the first generation Italian Americans, often making comments about all of the Italians in Frederick.

"Are you all signing up for my advanced trig class next year?" Mr. Grant asked the class.

Several people responded yes, and I turned to my friend Jerry and said, "Hell no. I am done with math."

"What is that, Giovanni?" Mr. Grant asked.

"No more math for me. I am going to law school. I don't need any more math." Yes, that was a cocky thing to say for sure, but I was just seventeen.

"You? Law school? Right," laughed Mr. Grant, mocking me.

Fuck him, I thought. My dad's words of encouragement popped into my mind. Don't let this guy bully you, I thought. We are not defined by our parents' limitations. My dad wasn't, and I won't be. Fuck him, I will show him.

Turns out, I did end up taking Mr. Grant's class—and got an A. Twenty years later, in 1984, I ran into him at a local grocery store. The exchange between us was burned into my brain.

"Giovanni, how are you?"

"Great, and you?"

"Very good, I just retired and am enjoying some freedom. What are you up to?"

"I am married, three kids. And I am a founding partner in a law firm in Boulder. Blessed."

I wonder if he remembered his hurtful words. Little did he know that he had motivated me, even if just a little bit.

"Wow, that is great."

^ ^ ^ ^ ^

My dad and Uncle Luciano worked their main jobs from nine o'clock in the morning to five o'clock in the afternoon and built homes during the nights and on weekends. This was the only life they knew, engrained in them from their upbringing. But my dad never complained, at least not in front of the children, and I got the impression he enjoyed the hard work. In the next few decades, he made great investment decisions and embodied the American dream. People like Mr. Grant did not limit him or me.

In my childhood, my dad told me stories about life during World War II and lectured me on many topics almost daily. Each had a lesson, and almost all included detailed descriptions of an almost mystical Cansano. In trying not to forget his past, he was trying to help form my future. But we were the weird family that butchered our food and spent every night and weekend together and whose children (especially the girls) were not allowed to do anything social with non-family. Unfortunately, the stories and lectures quickly grew old. "Dad, I know," I would say. "I have heard this story before." I did not really appreciate him and his struggles and efforts to make our lives better until our trip to Cansano.

CHAPTER EIGHT

First Impressions

As we enter the piazza, I immediately notice three large homes on the right. Unlike the homes in the rest of the town, these stone homes are grand and more like what you would see in Rome, built in Renaissance Revival style. The homes are surrounded by tall iron fences and trees, with rectangular windows covered by dark wood shutters. An old story emerges in my mind that I had long forgotten—or perhaps repressed—of how the Nazis set up command in one of these large homes during their occupation of the town in late 1943 and early 1944. At the time, the piazza became a place of horror. The villagers were stripped of their dignity, robbed and pillaged, enslaved, raped, and, ultimately, left to suffer and die. A chill runs down my spine as I remember the story. I want to ask about it, but the time doesn't seem right. I will ask later, I think to myself.

The home on the corner has been converted to an *albergo*, or hotel. On the left is the Catholic church, several shops, a bar, and then a row of homes leading to the municipal building, with a tree-lined park cutting a path between the homes on the right and left. Flowerpots and benches line the piazza. Over the next nine years, we visited many piazzas in other towns, but *Piazza XX Settembre* is the most charming and remains my favorite. Progress appeared to be slow, and the town has been forgotten by modern times. But the tranquility is thick, and I find myself feeling instantly connected to this place I have never before visited.

As we exit the piazza, which is only one block long, we turn right on *Via Casale*, and the architecture shifts. The homes are slightly more modern, rectangular, adorned with wooden doors and windows, and have small balconies with bright red, pink, yellow, and purple flowers hanging from ornate wrought iron railings. The doors and windows are arched. The homes, tightly packed like homes in San Francisco, are the colors of the local limestone straw, grey-green, pinkish salmon, stony grey, and limestone yellows and blues. Many of the homes had been renovated by first- or second-generation Italian Americans and Italian Canadians whose families were from here. Sprinkled among the remodeled are old, dilapidated homes abandoned after the deep recession that followed World War II. I study them carefully, wondering how bad it really was here in the late 1940s and early 1950s.

"Dad, what do '*affittare*' and '*vendere*' mean?" I ask, as we drive past several abandoned homes with those words on signs, already challenging my Italian.

"For rent and for sale," he replies. "The town has become empty. No one lives here."

Prior to World War II, about two thousand people lived in Cansano. By 2013, only three hundred people lived here. Later, I ask my Zio Pietro why this is the case. "The young have all moved to the big cities, as there is no work here," he replies in Italian. "The work here is farming and ranching, and the young are lazy. The locals have done nothing in recent years to keep the town going or vibrant." As we returned to Cansano and the surrounding areas over the next few years, I began to see what he meant. The other mountain towns in the region did a lot of reinvestment—rebuilding the town centers, incentivizing businesses, and attracting a mix of age groups and socioeconomic backgrounds. Cansano experienced some of this type of growth and revitalization between 2000 and 2009, with some Cansanesi returning to rebuild family properties and northern Italians and Europeans buying summer vacation fixer-upper properties in the quaint town to escape big city life. But the massive 2009 earthquake centered near L'Aquila in north Abruzzo damaged many homes in Cansano, including properties under construction, and Cansano's redevelopment halted. Even after the earthquake, nearby towns continued to focus on redevelopment, but for some reason, Cansano didn't, aside from a few summer and fall festivals. Cansano had become a strange mix of older locals like my uncle who never left after the war, a small group of twenty-year-olds ostensibly stuck in the town, and Cansanesi from the United States, Canada, and Australia who returned for brief visits.

Via Casale turns into *Via Roma*, and it takes only a minute to drive from the piazza to my cousin Rocco's bed-and-breakfast. While my uncle had been to the United States twice, I didn't really know him and had never had a meaningful conversation with him. This trip changed that, and he would become a special person in our lives. My uncle had arranged for the chauffeured van to pick us up at the airport in Rome for the two-hour drive east to Cansano. "I hope your uncle didn't spend too much on this," Aggie worried.

When we arrive, my uncle and his second wife, my cousin Rocco and his wife and two young daughters, and two helpers from the bed-and-breakfast greet us. After many hugs and kisses, we settle in for a large meal centered around *agnello*, freshly butchered lamb from my uncle's ranch just outside of town.

"Zio, I hope you didn't spend a lot of money on the van and driver," I say in Italian in a hesitant tone, not sure I was saying it right.

"Juwaa, you came to visit me for the first time, of course I am paying. It is my honor," he replies in Italian. "If I came to the United States, would you make me pay?"

"Yes, I would make you pay," I jokingly respond in Italian, and that was the start of a strong relationship.

My dad and Zio Pietro quickly get into their familiar cadence. They talk about politics and local issues plaguing Italy in general and Cansano specifically—no work ethic in the youth, poor government leadership, high taxes, and people leaving Italy for more opportunities. This is a conversation they have had many times before.

My dad urges my uncle to retire and sell his ranch.

"Why are you working so hard, for what?" Dad asks in Italian.

"Allora," my uncle responds emphatically, a word used by Italians in many sentences as a transition.

"Che posso fare! Non c'è nessuno a cui venderlo," he says.

I translate for Aggie and the kids: "What can I do? There is no one to sell it to."

As Dad and Zio Pietro catch up, I engage in an awkward and choppy conversation with my cousin and his family. I nervously try to carry out the conversation in Italian, something I haven't done in years. Translating back and forth for Aggie gives me some confidence, and I quickly immerse myself in three or four conversations with people around the table, all trying to communicate with each other, and me serving as a translator. Rocco and his daughters know some English, as it was required as part of their school curriculum.

After an excellent meal, Aggie is ready for bed at six p.m., tired from a long day of international travel. The rest of us walk down to the piazza, except for my uncle, who heads back to his ranch to make sure his eight hundred head of sheep are properly fed and readied for the night. Like my dad, Zio Pietro loved hard work. At eighty years of age, he still worked ten-plus hour days. He was fit, vibrant, full of energy, and looked like he was in his early sixties. And he was hip, wearing a backwards John Deere hat and Levi's while working the ranch and timeless Italian colors, textures, and layers when not working.

In later trips, Zio Pietro took me to his ranch and with him on his deliveries of lamb and pecorino cheese to local restaurants and markets. He—and only he—would deliver his products to his customers. He had the same charm and enchantment about him that my dad had.

In 2013, the walk to the piazza down a centuries-old cobblestone path surrounded by picturesque old homes was new to me. But I would come to do this same walk many times in subsequent trips, breathing in the crisp mountain air with a hint of sweet-smelling local timber that burned in the locals' fireplaces. And every time, profound, visceral feelings bubbled up from within—a connection to something spiritual buried deep inside me, something essential to the very foundation of who I am. I had no idea I was missing this feeling or how important it was to me.

CHAPTER NINE

La Passeggiata

The piazza is now busy and vibrant. A group of children play soccer along the street heading to the municipal building, and several clusters of people engage in conversation around the monument. People crisscross the piazza, catching up with one another.

The two restaurants are filled with people enjoying a glass of wine or a beer. The group of old men that I saw several hours earlier is still there; a few more men have joined them and their conversation is now even more animated. They are playing cards. A group of teens is in a small park just outside the piazza on the way to the cemetery.

This ritual, called the *passeggiata* (stroll), is one that happens every night in every city and town in Italy, usually before dinner, which Italians eat very late. All across Italy, it is the time to walk with family and friends, a time to socialize, eat, drink, and be seen. Each town has its own custom. In Siena, people walk from the *contrade* (neighborhoods) and circle the famous *Piazza del Campo*, where the *Palio di Siena* horse race is held twice a year. In Venice, locals and tourists walk the water-lined streets and stop in *barcaros* (appetizer-and-wine bars) and enjoy delicious *cicchetti* (bite-size appetizers) with an Aperol Spritz or wine.

And in the small towns like Cansano, it is all about the piazza. Some people dress for the occasion, especially on weekends when the *passeggiata* becomes the main social event. Men in their fedoras and women in bright dresses dot the piazza. This moment of sociability reinforces a sense of community for the townspeople. *La Passeggiata* is a vibrant social performance that allows people to mingle, gossip, and talk about news, politics, soccer, or family, weaving everyone into the fabric of the community. This is more than a simple walk—it is a cultural happening that celebrates the simple things in life: community, friendship, and sharing.

As we enter the piazza, my parents are quickly greeted by many of their old friends. It has been fifteen years since they were last here, and they are overcome with memories and emotions as they catch up with people they have not seen in many years, including some people that they have not seen since the 1950s.

This was my father's element. He was a social butterfly, and he loved to talk. During this trip and our return trip in 2014 I watched this scene play out many times—my father engaged in joyful conversation with old friends he had not seen in years or perfect strangers he had just met. Whether he ran into his godfather in Campo di Giove, an old friend in the remote mountain town of Scanno that he had not seen in decades, a shop owner in Praiano that he had never met, my uncle's ranch hands, or Cansanese old-timers whom he saw daily, my father would stop and talk. About anything and everything, and with a smile. Emiliano was an "everyman," and he was comfortable talking about any topic, whether it was the stock market, politics, hunting and fishing, food, sports, winemaking, music, gambling, or everyday life. As a child, I watched him befriend many people with his charm, wisdom, and gift of gab.

As a teenager, I was embarrassed, really for no reason other than impatience and immaturity. "Dad, let's go," I would say. As I grew older, I came to appreciate and learn from my dad's chatty quality. And I was ashamed about having been embarrassed by him.

While he was certainly opinionated, Dad was comfortable talking to and befriending anyone—from CEOs, to friends of my sisters and me, to those from every walk of life that entered his grocery store in the '80s and '90s. People just gravitated to him. He had that "it" charm, yet he was humble. Just like Cansano.

Rocco, his seven-year-old daughter Flavia, Donato, Izabella, and I sit at a table in the outdoor seating area in front of the bar, and we order wine for Rocco and me and Italian sodas for the children. My parents make their way around the piazza, talking to everyone they know. As I watch, I am reminded of an old postcard my parents had from Cansano. In the United States, my parents framed it and hung it outside my childhood bedroom. It was undated and showed hundreds of Cansanese socializing in the piazza. In the photo, a few scooters are lined up on the left, and a green Fiat is on the front right of the picture. I always assumed it was from the early or late 1950s. Men were dressed in suits and women in dresses, and as a child I wondered what they were celebrating each time I walked by the picture. Sitting and watching the Piazza with my own two eyes, I wonder if the old postcard was just a picture of the nightly *passeggiata* in Cansano.

After several hours and many glasses of wine and greetings with very friendly strangers, we saw Flavia, who had run back to my Zio's house, re-emerge and announce, "*Cena è pronta*!"

"Dinner at nine p.m.? Didn't we already eat dinner?" I ask Rocco in Italian.

"No, that was a snack," he chuckles in broken English.

"Here the custom is to eat dinner at eight or nine p.m. after the nightly walk," he says in Italian.

And so, we head back for our second dinner. Aggie, fully clothed, is passed out on the bed from the long day of travel. We are exhausted, but I don't want to be disrespectful. After a multiple-course meal of local sautéed vegetables, prosciutto, mortadella, salami, cheese, pasta, and lamb—and more wine—I collapse in bed. What a first day.

CHAPTER TEN

Our First Walk

Does an old monument with names engraved in Italian marble define you? Do abandoned homes once filled with the daily sounds of ancestors' lives help form you? I had never been to Cansano before and the stories I had heard seemed disconnected from me and my daily life. The difficulties, pain, and suffering of the post-World War II era and subsequent immigrant life were not mine. Yet, after one day, I wanted to touch and get to know this place of origin, and I would soon have an awakening, an understanding of where—and from whom—I came.

There is no better way to get to know a town or city than to walk it and talk to its people. I didn't grasp that until this trip; in the years to come, I always made time in my day to walk the streets of places I visited for work or fun.

I am a morning person. My clock always adjusts to the time zone I am in, and I always wake up around five a.m., often earlier. On our second day in Cansano, I quietly leave my room, not wanting to wake Aggie. The chilly, crisp air greets me as I walk out and turn up the street. The local trees and plants emit a distinct fragrance that is new to me. I see my dad sitting on a bench near my cousin's *agriturismo*, which is a farm-to-table bed-and-breakfast-style home that he rents to tourists and Cansanesi returning to the old country. A small drinking fountain is in front of the bench with a small trickle of water gurgling from the spout.

"You are up too," he says upon seeing me. *"Buongiorno."*

"*Buongiorno*. I get up early every day," I reply.

Behind the bench where my dad sits is an open area with no homes; in the distance, I see a railroad bridge with five arches buried in the trees and mountains in the background. Past the open field are homes that surround the piazza below with the bridge set off in the distance behind it.

After a moment of silence, my dad says, "Your mom's old house is right there." He points to a home across the street.

The ninety-year-old two-story home is in great condition, and I wonder how my grandfather Panfilo afforded it.

"A Ruscitti lives there now," my dad points out. Dark shutters manicure the windows and multicolored plants fill several pots in front of the home.

"Is the water safe to drink?" I ask my dad, looking at the fountain. The fountain looks weathered. "I can't believe it still works. Where does the water come from?"

"Of course it still works. It was made with quality," he responds, standing up to have a sip and to prove that he is right. "This was here in the 1950s."

"Quality." For my father, anything Italian or made in Italy is the best. Cars, clothing, food, wine, engineering, music, art—everything. "You know, America was named after an Italian, Amerigo Vespucci," he has said on many occasions. Whenever we drove over roads or bridges in a state of disrepair, he would say, "Look at this junk. In Italy, the roads and bridges are built to last." It didn't matter what it was, it probably originated in Italy or was made better in Italy, according to my father. He told anyone who would listen, and his charm didn't make it offensive. In fact, I heard this remark so much that, as a six-year-old, I asked my mom if Jesus was Italian as we watched the credits roll at the end of the movie *The Ten Commandments* and I saw all of the Italian names come across the screen. She laughed, "Maybe." My mom still tells that story.

"Do you want some coffee?" I ask.

"*Va bene*," he replies. "Sounds good." We head down to the dining room in the *agriturismo*.

No one is up yet, so we make some espresso and Dad eats a pastry his brother had picked up for us. My dad loved his Italian pastries; this was the standard Italian *colazione*, or breakfast: espresso and a cookie or pastry.

We don't say much, which unfortunately had become our norm before this 2013 trip. But being here in my father's hometown would change that.

"Do you want to walk to the piazza?" he asks.

"Sure," I say.

The air is crisp and it is still dark out. For the first time in my life, I notice the lights. *Via Roma* is lined with vintage, cast-iron streetlights that light up the path. They are not the bright, clear lights I am accustomed to, but they are warm and soothing, amber in color. As we walk down the street, my dad is quiet and pensive, and I feel that he is reminiscing about his childhood. As we approach the piazza, he tells me who used to live in the homes, many now abandoned. Names I had heard but people I didn't know. The homes are many different terracotta colors and all made of rock and/or limestone. The main entries have arched wooden doors with each arch decorated with irregularly shaped stones. All of the buildings are two or three stories high, and each has rectangular windows or doors on every level, many with small balconies. Many of the homes had been recently renovated by old Cansanese families who wanted to stay connected with their past.

The piazza is completely empty, and we walk to the monument, past the old and abandoned *barcaro* named *Vino e birra*. "Your grandfathers, especially Panfilo, loved having drinks here," my dad says. A dark grey cobblestone street forms the border of the piazza, transitioning to pinkish colored cobblestones around the fallen soldier monument. The pinkish cobblestones are formed in arched patterns, with white cobblestones mixed in. The warm lights around the piazza softly illuminate numerous pots filled with colorful local plants and several wood benches around the monument. On the horizon, I see a park on the right where the teenagers were the night before and more Roman palazzi-style homes on the left on the road leading to Pescocostanzo.

We stop at the monument and I read the names—Morelli, Ruscitti, Villani, D'Orazio, DiGiallonardo, De Angelis.

"Dad, are these our relatives?" I ask.

"Some, yes," he says. "Everyone was related somehow. The poor men volunteered for the wars to make money for their families. Life was hard, and they did what they had to do. It was not like today."

That was a common phrase he used: "It was not like today."

Over the next hour or so, the sun slowly rises and layers of sunlight cascade over the limestone buildings and red rock shingles, creating shadows and glows I have never before seen. We walk the road, which is lined with thick trees, from the piazza to the municipal building. A little park edges the street on the left, with green park benches and flowers. Most of the homes in this part of town are occupied and well-maintained. At the end of the road is the municipal building. It is a deep dark yellow, light orangish two-story building. The Italian flag hangs from a second story balcony, and the town crest sits above the main entry.

"This is where I went to school, to fifth grade," Dad reminds me.

His sentences dance in and out of Italian and English.

"*L'insegnante si chiamava Beniamin Collechia* (The teacher was named Beniamin Collechia). *Un buon uomo* (A good man). *Ma* (But)—A good man, but he was strict—he would hit us *alle mani* (on the hands), the knuckles, with—what do you call it?—a wood ruler. *Lui mi ha fatto imparare bene l'aritmetica* (He made me learn arithmetic very well)."

I was always amazed by my father's math skills. He could do any math problem, no matter how complex, in his head, in seconds. When my sisters and I were children, he would test us with a math problem. We would do it on paper or with a calculator, and he would do it in his head. He always beat us to the answer and his was always right.

"If only I could have gotten the education you got, I could have really been something," he says.

"*Ma, io non avevo quelle opportunità*" (But, I didn't have those opportunities)."

"Dad, what are you talking about?" I ask him. "For me to make the same level of progress you made, I would have to become a billionaire."

Guilt comes over me. My dad did not pay for any of my education—not my undergrad, my MBA, or my law degree. I had to work hard for those degrees with student loans and numerous odd jobs (and while I was in law school, Aggie worked seven days a week), and I vowed to make sure my children graduated debt-free, even as I was still paying off my debt. Yes, there was some resentment on my end. But paying for my college education was not part of my dad's reality. He had no formal education and no real exposure to the American tradition of paying for your children's education. In his world, a man was responsible for his own path and if I chose college, an MBA, and a law degree, I would pay for it. At age eighteen, my father had to make bigger decisions than where to go to college. He had to decide when to leave Italy and start a new life in a new country. Standing together with my father that June morning in Cansano, I realize that he has given me so many opportunities that he didn't have. I was about to appreciate that even more over the next hour.

We walk most of the old part of town—from the municipal building down a steep and zigzagging sidewalk named *Via Civitella* through a completely abandoned part of town leading to a water fountain with the date 1891 and the town crest inscribed in the stone. Over a door, the year 1822 is inscribed. Many of the doors are very short.

"Those are *le stalle* (the stalls) where families kept *gli animali* (their animals)," he says, mixing Italian and English words in the same sentence.

As we reach the fountain, he says, "This is where the women and girls would come to get water. They filled the jugs and carried them back to their homes on their heads."

As I think about my mom doing this, he adds, "And the women would do laundry here, too. Not washing machines like today. They would fill a bucket, not the same ones for drinking water, and hand-wash the clothes. Little or no soap. Just water and stones to get the dirt out. You don't know what we went through in them days."

We continue on our walk, up a gradual hill with a great view of the valley to Sulmona below, down another wider street to another fountain. From here, we walk up to *Via Due Porte*, the street where my father's family lived. While it was called a street, it was really a cobblestone path or sidewalk. There are no people out this morning and, aside from our conversation, the only other sounds are loud crunching sounds each step make on the cobblestones and birds chirping in the decaying homes. Small stray cats scurry around the area, while others sit in protection of their adopted home. Later, we learned that stray cats occupy many of the cities and villages, especially in central and southern Italy. Many are spayed and neutered by caring volunteers, and all over Italy, including in Cansano, you will see containers with leftover pasta for the cats.

The stone homes were abandoned long ago and were falling apart. Floors in the homes—as well as entire roofs on many homes—were caved in. Doors were missing and some of the windows had wood shutters. Overgrown trees and bushes protruded through some of the doors and windows. The steep cobblestone sidewalks that parted the homes were largely intact, and a few balconies cast slight shadows over the path below.

It occurs to me that, while I had heard so much about this area, I had not seen any pictures of it. Pictures would not have done it justice anyway. I have never seen anything like this, and I am struck by the beauty of the architecture of the homes and the backdrop of the cloud-covered Maiella mountains, which somehow overshadow the overwhelming sadness that I feel looking at the state of the homes.

"They don't make homes like this anymore," Dad says.

"How old are they?" I ask.

"Hundreds of years old. Some older," he replies.

As we walk up the steep street, I wonder how the women made this daily trek with water on their heads. Dad points out a few homes that had the year they were built engraved in the limestone walls, the marker barely visible: "1732" reads one home, "1686" reads another.

"Them days, you know the people building the houses, they don't have the cement like they do today. Cement was very sparse, and they didn't have the money, the price was probably much higher, so they buy the lime," Dad says. "You had to cook the rocks."

"What?" I ask. "Cook rocks?"

"That is right. So, they have some special rocks. The older people, they knew what kinds of rocks to get. You dig around and you go deep about six to eight feet or depends how big, and you make the hole big enough and you build the wall with the rocks about one to two meters. We go up on the hill, on the north side there was a lot of wood, lots of branches. You need a lot of wood to support the fire. It could take a few weeks to cook the rocks. You go up on the hill, cut the branch, then a bunch of men would split the money when they sell the lime."

"Wow," I say. I had heard this before, but it didn't register, like many of his stories.

"To cook the rocks, it took a lot of fire, it created a lot of ash, and the poor men would work day and night. When the rocks were done, they would close it up and let the rocks cool off for about a week. Then they could go uncover all of the rocks and uncover the lime and sell the lime. The rock would start to boil again with added water, and it would create a cream. Once it was all creamy, like ricotta, they used that to build the house and everything else. Or they used it to paint the house. We make different colors. We had no paint them days. And these last forever. Look, eighty years later and the paint is still there."

Paint. A memory surfaces. In the mid-1970s my dad's and uncle's construction company was building a new home in Longmont, Colorado. A large department store named Gibson's was closing its Longmont location. One Saturday morning, Dad, Uncle Luciano, my cousin Franco, and I went into the store to see if there were any deals. They were always looking for deals. We had been there the weekend before and the store was running a "50 percent off" sale. Today, it was 70 percent off and "everything must go." We walked into the paint department, which was still fully stocked with hundreds, if not thousands, of cans of paint of all sizes, colors, and types.

My dad walked up to a clerk, a pimple-faced teen, and said, "Give me 90 percent off and we will take it all."

"Sir, I cannot do that," he shyly responded. "I can give you 70 percent off."

"OK, fine, we are leaving. Keep it all," my dad responded in a loud, aggressive tone. I felt for the kid. Here we go again, I thought. I had seen this act before.

My uncle jumped in, on cue, and said, "How about 80 percent?" The kid had no clue what had just happened to him.

"Ummm, let me call my manager," he said. The deal was done.

Franco and I spent the rest of that Saturday and Sunday making numerous trips to Gibson's with our fathers to load the paint into their two pickup trucks. Even though they constructed numerous homes over the next few years and used the paint on each, hundreds of cans of the paint (certainly dust by now), still sit in my parents' garage.

"Dad, we really need to throw this away," I suggested to my father more than forty years later. "It is not good."

"Why?" he responded. "It was a good deal and some of it may be good." Not likely, I thought.

^ ^ ^ ^ ^

Back in Cansano in 2013, my dad stops in front of his father Rocco's childhood home.

"This is where my dad lived as a boy. And right there is where I lived," he says, pointing to a small home on the right about thirty yards up the sidewalk.

"Cassiodoro," he says. "That was my grandfather. *D'oro* (of gold) was his nickname. He was a big man, very generous."

I wonder what his life must have been like. I had never heard anything about him and want to ask about his life. Unfortunately, I don't, as I am mesmerized by the views.

As I start walking into the arched entry to my grandfather's childhood home, my father urges me to be careful.

"You shouldn't go in there," he parents. "Not safe."

The entry to my grandfather Rocco's childhood home is covered with spiderwebs, and it has been several decades since anyone walked up through the doorway, which has two decaying wood doors that hang precariously on their hinges, and up the limestone stairs on the other side. The home is several hundred years old, yet the craftsmanship and attention to detail strikes me, as I notice that each step has an overhanging lip. The seven or eight stairs are covered with debris, rocks, and pieces of wood that had fallen from the ceiling. On the top of the staircase is a pinkish limestone landing, and the window that once protected the home from the elements is caved in, revealing a small courtyard overgrown with vegetation. As I slowly turn to my left, I see the inside of the home. The two rooms that are visible are small, with some of the walls painted a greenish lime color. A fireplace with darkened stone is built into a wall, the clear focal point of the room. Sunlight lights up each room, pouring through large holes in the roof, and I remember family life as my father described it many times.

"At the time, we didn't have a furnace. We didn't have anything to warm up or cool off the house. Cooking—we had the chimney, built the fire, and then you have a hook on the top of the fire. You would use that to make the water boil; you would make the roast using the steam. That's the way it was."

I remember this description as I see the hook hanging in the fireplace.

As I exit my grandfather's home, we walk toward my dad's childhood home, which is less than thirty yards up the steep staircase. My dad tells me about each home and who lived there.

"These were all Ruscittis on this side," he says, pointing to the left.

"Above our home lived my best friend, Concetto Morelli, and his family."

His voice is strong, but I can tell he is fighting back emotions. "We all lived in that little home." He continues, "The house belonged to my grandfather Pietro, but he gave it to my mom and dad when they got married."

My dad was the middle child of five children, and I couldn't imagine how they all survived living in such a small house, with another large family right above them. "They were good times, but they were hard." Again, themes he often repeated.

The door was blocked with weeds and plants, so we could not enter his childhood home. "I will show you another time," he says. Unfortunately, my dad was not able to do so, only making it back one more time for our second trip in 2014. The entry was still blocked.

(In a bittersweet moment, during a trip back to Cansano in 2017, Dante and I entered my father's abandoned home in *La Partayova* and saw old hooks hanging from the ceiling, reminding me of my grandfather Panfilo's wine cellar in Frederick and of the winemaking days with my dad and grandfather.)

"Dad, what happened here?" I ask. "Why is this part of town in this condition?"

"*La guerra*," he said of World War II. "We lost everything."

"Who owns this land?" I ask.

"We do."

CHAPTER ELEVEN

My Grandfathers

In 2018, my sons Dante and Donato received a gift—time to spend with their grandfather and to listen to and hear him. They recorded him telling stories that he had told me my whole life. My dad loved telling stories, teaching and mentoring, and he loved spending time with his grandchildren, especially Dante and Donato, who truly listened to him.

"I miss my community," Dad told Dante, "because I have the memories of my younger age. We didn't have no money to go around. We spent time in the community. We got together as family and friends. My friends were like brothers."

He paused and then added, "How do you describe that? It's tough growing up as a child in misery, but we made the best of what we could during the war and after it ended."

Italy entered World War II in June 1940 as one of the Axis powers. Like many fascist leaders, Benito Mussolini preyed on the suffering of the undereducated broken men and women with promises of hope and help for the poor people through jobs and the building of roads, infrastructure, and rail lines. Using newspapers, radio, art, the cinema, posters, and the education system (which began the indoctrination process in the first grade), Mussolini misled the people, especially poorer peasants in small communities, into buying his populist beliefs—a model that would repeat itself in history many times, including as I write this book. Italians were supposed to see Mussolini and his party as the conduit through which

Italy was to enter a future of prosperity and power. While he provided some jobs and built an infrastructure within the country, he took away so much more and eventually led the country, including the people of Cansano, through pure hell.

World War II did not initially impact Cansano. Life went on as usual. "We lived our lives as normal and it was a good life," my father said. "Until November 1943."

The industrialization of Italy had not fully reached Cansano by the early '40s when my parents were young children, and Mussolini's promises went unfulfilled. At the time, like many of its sister towns in Abruzzo, Cansano was a poor farming community. While there were some advancements—a railroad connecting the town to Sulmona and other towns to the south, a clean water fountain system that relied on gravity and channeled water from an aquifer in a closed system to provide pressure, and electricity in parts of the town—sewage systems did not exist and homelife was still somewhat primitive. The people of the ancient village were forced to create a living in the rugged mountains surrounding Cansano. While the land was rich in timber and wild walnut, fig, and cherry and plum trees, farming was difficult.

"Each family had a small plot of land here and there," my father often told me with his thumb pressed near the top of his index finger to emphasize the point. "It wasn't like the farms in the United States. All that land and machinery. We had nothing motorized and used our hands and donkeys. And we grew what we could. It was a simple life."

As we stand before Dad's childhood house on this cool June 2013 morning, I remember the stories and, looking at the terrain, I wonder to myself where the land was and how they possibly could have farmed it. The valley down below the homes was steep and dense with trees. On the other side of the valley was a steep mountain with more rocks and trees.

"Dad, where did you own land to farm?" I ask, leaving my earlier question about what happened to the neighborhood open and unanswered.

"I don't remember exactly where," he responds. "Here and there."

The homes in the old part of town, *La Partayova*, were originally built in a row for safety from thieves and vagrants who traveled from town to town in medieval times taking what wasn't theirs. Later, the architecture provided protection from the brutal mountain winters and heavy snow. More importantly, it allowed families the ability to support one another. Some had wheat and corn, others had animals, some had ovens for baking, and some had wood. "It was a community," my father often told me. "We all helped each other." He tells me that again this morning.

When I was a young boy my dad took me everywhere. I remember him taking me to the building that once served as the old grocery store in Frederick on Fifth Street. The building was abandoned and the owner, the son of an Italian immigrant, wanted to remodel it. He was a college professor and knew nothing about construction. My dad helped, for free, for months after work or on weekends. On innumerable other occasions, he helped the older Cansanese families in Frederick or other Italian immigrants in Denver with little projects in their homes, including fixing up bathrooms, installing kitchen cabinets and appliances, painting, remodeling, repairing wine cellars, making wine, pressing prosciutto, and repairing fences. I was always in his hip pocket during these projects, grabbing his tools and helping when and where I could. Mostly, the old women pinched my cheeks and fed me soda and Italian cookies.

"*Mangia, mangia, sei troppo magro*," they would say. "Eat, eat, you are too skinny."

I wasn't, but to them, unless I was chubby, I was skinny. And chubby was preferred by the old Italian ladies.

We continue walking; I wonder if any of the old Cansanesi I knew in Frederick lived in these deserted homes, and Dad shakes his head, a memory surfacing.

"We used to play simple games right here."

"We had no toys at all," my dad told my son in 2018 during one of their recorded sessions, when describing his childhood and the area. "Growing up, the kids would go play outside, and we would make up games in the middle of the street," he continued, referring to the steep stairwell on *Via Due Porte*. "We would get some flat rocks, some bricks, and make up games."

I had heard this story also, and I think about it as my father and I climb the now-empty and quite steep staircase in *La Partayova*. He often told me that staircase was full of life in the early 1940s.

As we walk, Dad says, "Look at this area. Nothing left. *Che peccato* (what a shame)." We pause and the words hang in the air.

He continues, "When I was young, the men, they walked up and down the pathway all day, some with their cattle or sheep or goats. Others with the wood or crops they harvested."

He shakes his head, and then continues, "And the women, they worked very hard. They carried water up the stairs from the fountains below town in a pot they held on their heads. You would see the women, with the kids all around them, carrying the laundry that they washed in the river. It wasn't like today with washing machines. And some women, like your grandma Filomena and your grandma Nunziata, they took care of the animals in the stables, and they brought the milk and eggs back to the homes."

I look around the now-deserted and neglected area and picture life back then. For a moment, I wonder if that way of life brought more joy and happiness to people than the craziness of today's busy world full of iPhones, social media, and sitting behind a desk pushing paper.

"The men and women worked together, doing their part," my dad says as we walk up the staircase. "But they would stop and talk. It was a community, very safe."

In her book *La Pittoresca Terra di Cansano*, Cansanese Nicolina D'Orazio Di Tunno, described the area in the late '30s and '40s as follows:

> Cansano was therefore a composite social body, not an agglomeration of houses. It was a small world of work, daily struggles, of faces, of encounters, of quarrels, of loves, voices, and songs. In this environment, small events marked the life of simple and humble men and women.

This was the community Dad remembered, missed, and described to Dante in 2018.

"After the games with rocks, the kids, we would feed the chickens and other animals. Five-, six-, and seven-year-olds all did that. That is what you do. Help the family," he continues as we climb the stairs.

"Some days, when I was young, me and my brothers would go watch the sheep for my dad so he could work," my father often told me. "Other days, we went to school. But we had to help the family first."

Both of my grandfathers were hardworking laborers, doing whatever work they could find in the late 1930s and early 1940s to feed their young families. My father often spoke of his father with reverence. "He was good to us kids. Unless he drank too much, then he was a little crazy." Many of the men from the World War II generation were like this, perhaps trying to forget the shame the war caused and their inability to protect their families. My grandfather Rocco died the year before I was born, only one year after finally immigrating to Frederick from Cansano.

"My dad, for a living, cut wood, planted wheat and corn so we would have food for the whole year," my dad described his father. "You didn't have enough wheat and corn to sell, only enough for your family. The same for animals. We had only enough for us."

Families stored wheat, corn, nuts, pickled vegetables, and dried fruits in the cool basements of their homes. Wheat was used to make bread and pasta and corn to make polenta. Meats were cured. "A delicacy was dried sausage that was bottled in lard and used during the year for sandwiches and flavoring for the pasta and polenta," he said.

My father shows me where they stored these items in some of the homes as we walk that morning, and I remember us making the same bottled sausage that we stored in our damp and dusk basement in my first home on Sixth Street in Frederick.

"The only way my dad could make money was by cutting wood and selling it. The cords of wood were about a meter long, and those poor men, in the fall, would go into the mountains, with a hatchet, maybe a donkey, and they would cut what they could. Go into Sulmona or Pacentro and sell what they could," he says of his father and many other Cansanese.

While many men worked in the nearby limestone quarries and a few worked as blacksmiths, tailors, and shoemakers in the piazza, others, like my grandfather Rocco, were lumberjacks. The only item of abundance in the area was wood—beech, oak, pine, and ash—and it offered a form of currency that made survival possible for men like Rocco. My grandfather would rise early and ready his mule, pack a saddlebag of bread, fruit and nuts, a flask of water, and a hatchet. Sometimes alone, sometimes in a group, he would harvest his load and head to Sulmona where he would sell the wood for money or trade it for oil, sugar, tomatoes, legumes, garlic, onions, and other items that could not be grown in Cansano. And then he would hike back to Cansano.

"He would make money by making the cords of wood. The wood was about a meter long, and was very heavy," Dad told Dante in 2018. "The poor men, in the fall, they go cut the wood, and the good men knew what they were doing and do two cords a day using a hatchet. You better believe they were strong. Them days they had the real food though. The food we made was from plants and the earth, not the chemicals you have today."

As Dad and I walk up *La Partayova* that June morning, he tells me a similar story and a memory emerges from my early teenage years. The idea of paying for firewood would never have crossed my father's mind. Not with his upbringing. Trees were in abundance and they belonged to everyone. In 1978, he built his home in Frederick, which included a large fireplace in the living room. The fireplace was made from moss-covered rocks that we collected from the mountains between Lyons and Berthoud, Colorado. We spent many Saturdays and Sundays in 1977 and 1978 driving to the mountains to find the moss-covered rocks for the fireplace. We gathered so many rocks that many still sit in Dad's yard today. On numerous occasions between my eighth and tenth grade years, and after a full day of school and a long and grueling football practice, I, my dad, my uncle Luciano and my cousin Franco would drive up to Brainard Lake, which was about a ninety-minute drive one way. Using hatchets, we cut drying and dried-out trees for our fireplaces for the year and dragged them back to our trucks parked along the road. "This is good for the forest," Dad would say. My mom and Aunt Bianca packed dinners for us, usually some pasta with red sauce and sausage and meatballs or assorted panini with prosciutto, different dried salami, and provolone cheese. Before driving back home, we ate our dinners with a glass of my dad's homemade wine. We collected so much firewood those years that, like the rocks, many cords still sit in my dad's backyard.

That June morning in Cansano, I wonder how many of my friends did similar things with their dads. And I think about my dad and his father.

While my grandfather Rocco was a lumberjack, my mom's dad, Panfilo, and his father, Falco, were trained to build kilns, which were used to make lime for building homes. This craft put them in high demand, and they made more money than the lumberjacks. This was how my grandfather afforded the nice home with the stunning balcony I had seen earlier on that June 2013 morning.

I think about stories of my grandfather Panfilo in Italy traveling from town to town looking for work, sometimes staying in the towns with family or friends for weeks at a time. Unlike with my grandfather Rocco, I was fortunate to get to know and spend a lot of time with my grandfather Panfilo. He lived a few blocks away from us in Frederick, and I spent most summer days with him in the late 1970s and early 1980s before his death in 1982. Like my dad, he was a social man and took me with him to his favorite restaurant and bar, Pete's Place, which was owned by a fellow Cansanese. Many of the older, retired Cansanesi men in Frederick spent their days there drinking wine, playing cards or bocce, cooking for each other, and telling stories about the "old country," and he took me with him many times. I was ten, eleven, and twelve, and I loved watching and listening to the old men tell their stories. Just like the men I saw in the piazza in Cansano.

My grandfather Panfilo was captured by the Nazis early in World War II and had to execute a dangerous escape—he dug a short tunnel in the mountains with a fellow Cansanese to escape his captors. He never talked about life in the old country. After arriving in Colorado in 1954, he never returned to Italy, not even when my mom flew back to Italy in 1957 to marry my father. Maybe his memories were too painful. Maybe he was trying to forget. But I never asked about his experience in Italy, which I now regret.

"They worked very hard, like donkeys," my dad described my grandfathers. Hard work was another common theme in my dad's stories.

"We had no electricity, and it was cold. But we knew nothing else, so we didn't know what we didn't have. We were happy. But that was before the war," he often told me.

"It was simple and we were happy, even though we had *nothing*," he said, emphasizing the word "nothing" with intensity in his thick Italian accent.

"Everyone sat around the fireplace telling stories about the fairies or the ghosts—lots of ghost stories. In the primitive days, the people they go steal—the gold and so on—they had the stories about people getting killed over the treasure and then followed the stories about the ghosts. Everyone would listen and sometimes you would dream at night. They were scary for kids," Dad described for Dante.

One ghost story he told numerous times, including on our morning walk in June 2013:

> My dad was in the army. He told me the story about a time he came back from the military, the train came back and stopped in Sulmona. He had to wait for the morning train back to Cansano. So, he had to walk about 12 kilometers back to Cansano in the middle of the night. He reached this fountain along the way and finds an old man—a relative—sitting by the fountain. He says, "Uncle Nick, what are you doing over here?"
>
> Uncle Nick said, "Oh my son, it got a little bit late and I'm tired, just resting a bit."
>
> My dad suggested that they walk back together. So, they start to walk and they were talking all along.
>
> They reach close to where we used to live.

My dad pauses in the story and points to his old house and continues:

When they reach it, the old man says, "Rocco, you go home, nephew, and I will talk to you tomorrow morning."

My dad responds, "I'll wait for you."

"No, go home. It is late," Nick says. The next morning, he gets up and goes to see Uncle Nick's wife and asks if Nick had made it home safely.

She says, "Oh, my son, he's dead!"

"He's dead?" my dad repeated, shocked. "But we walked together last night from Sulmona."

"Oh no, no, no. He died a few years ago," she said.

My childhood was similar. Our families were close, literally and figuratively, and we spent weekends together picnicking in Rocky Mountain National Park, making wine and prosciutto, playing bingo and other games, and telling ghost stories. My family loved their stories about spirits. It was a big part of their Catholic religious beliefs. Catholicism is clear on the existence of a soul that survives the body, an accounting before God, and an eternal condition in either heaven or hell. They also believe in purgatory, a place or condition for the soul that has passed personal judgment but still has the temporal component of sins to atone for before going to heaven.

On many of my walks through the Cansano area in the years that followed, I sensed those spirits. For me, it wasn't religious, as I had long ago abandoned the need to follow a structured religion and practices that I believed were actually contrary to the teachings of many religions and that invited judgment and prejudice. Instead, it was spiritual and part of my personal evolution in my late forties and early fifties. My trips to Cansano were a huge part of this and were a source of calm for me.

Our childhood gatherings were a study in family dynamics. My family did everything with passion, emotion, loudness, and, inevitably, some arguing and yelling. Somebody was always upset with and not talking to someone else. "If so-and-so is there, I am not going." Maybe it was a result of having grown up in tight quarters in Cansano. Maybe it was their culture. Or maybe it was just who they were. But the arguments and yelling were always quickly forgotten.

As we walk up *Via Due Porte* through *La Partayova* back to my uncle's house that June 2013 morning, these stories come flooding back to me, taking form and having context. My dad's struggles and accomplishments take on new meaning: arriving in the United States at age twenty-one with just the suit on his back and a fifth grade Italian education, speaking no English and working below-minimum-wage jobs, retiring at age sixty-two as a multimillionaire. I was starting to understand what he had long been telling me.

CHAPTER TWELVE

Hank

Hank was my first real pet. He was a red-haired golden retriever that Dante, Donato, and I picked out of a litter of eight puppies. I had a "pet" rabbit when I was five or six years old, but we butchered it for Easter Sunday dinner. We had been raising it for the occasion. But I didn't know and named it Peter Cotton Tail.

Hank and I shared the same birthday; he and I were buddies. When he was a puppy, I took him on runs. As years passed and Hank and I got older and Hank's hips developed dysplasia, our runs turned into early morning walks. My dad always tried to feed Hank people food. And Hank knew it. He always begged my dad for food, knowing he would cave.

"Dad, don't do that. I don't want him to get sick," I said every time my parents visited.

"What are you talking about?" Dad replied. "He is a dog. He can eat everything."

On December 4, 2016, my parents drove the thirty minutes from their home to ours to say goodbye to then-fourteen-year-old Hank. We were putting him down the next morning. My dad brought him a toy, something he did every time he visited. They, too, were good buddies.

"Emilio, we bought a rotisserie chicken for you to feed Hank," Aggie told my dad.

"It is about time you fed him good food. Not that junk out of a bag. You can feed him anything. All the leftovers."

I watched Dad feed Hank the roasted chicken for his last dinner, and I cannot tell who was happier, Hank or my dad, giggling as he fed him.

Later, as they prepared to leave, Dad leaned over to pet Hank. He started to tear up. "I love you, Hank. You are a good boy."

Aggie and I looked at each other. I was fifty years old at the time; my father had never said "I love you" to me. Not because he didn't love me. But because it wasn't what men from his generation said.

Several years later, we started saying "I love you" to each other.

CHAPTER THIRTEEN

The Nazi Invasion

A family's present condition, future, and history can change in an instant, and sometimes the impact is not known for years to come. For my family, that instant was on November 11, 1943. Italy's declaration of war on Britain and France on June 10, 1940—almost seventy-three years to the day before my first trip to my ancestral home—put in motion a series of events that culminated with a horrific, unexpected Nazi occupation of many small towns in Abruzzo that no one was prepared for or expected. This occupation changed my family's condition—as it did that of so many other Cansanesi—from a manageable level of poverty and scarcity to famine, hopelessness, despair, loss, and suffering. And these words don't describe the actual conditions. This led to mass immigration, prejudice and judgment, and additional poverty, but this time in new lands of Australia, Canada, and the United States. Ultimately, hard labor, persistent dreams, and opportunity helped them realize the immigrant's dream. The seven-month period between November 1943 and June 1944, as well as the post-war years spent attempting to recover from that episode, would create a resiliency and bond, expressed by a tradition of hospitality, kindness, knowing, and understanding, between the Cansanesi people and their descendants. It also created a culture of frugality, discipline, entrepreneurialism, and industriousness that shaped generations of Cansanese that I grew up with in Frederick.

And it all started with the ego, greed, and desire for power that drove the Italian leaders, in particular Mussolini and his son-in-law, Galeazzo Ciano. But first, some World War II history, mostly learned from my dad with some from my uncles, other Cansanese, and history books:

By early 1943, the Nazi and Italian forces were losing ground in the war, having lost battles in Greece and North Africa, which were particularly important fronts for the Axis and especially Italy. The Allies were also planning to attack the Axis through the Italian peninsula. Mussolini's son-in-law, who was the head of Italy's foreign ministry, sensed defeat and urged his father-in-law to join the Allies, which incensed Mussolini and eventually led to the collapse of his regime. Numerous versions of the story exist, but this is what my father told me: Ciano, whose own father helped form the Italian National Fascist Party in early 1921—the party that Mussolini would eventually take over the following year—urged Mussolini to join Hitler against the Allies early in World War II, reasoning that it would be good to be part of the winning side. According to some historians and my father, Mussolini despised Hitler, but he was entranced by power, which inspired Mussolini to believe he could use Hitler to complete his fascist vision of replicating the Roman empire. He followed Ciano's advice and declared war against France and England. It was a bad move, as Italy's military was ill-prepared for what it was about to face.

"The son-in-law, he was the real bad one," said my father.

So, the story goes that Ciano began doubting the Hitler allegiance in early 1941 when the Nazis invaded Poland without advising Ciano, and he urged his father-in-law to switch to the Allies side. But it was too late. Italy's fate was decided, and it set in motion a series of events that eventually impacted the Abruzzo region, Cansanesi, and my family.

Concerned he might be a traitor and believing that he was quitting on the Italian people, Mussolini removed his son-in-law as foreign minister. Ciano became ambassador to the Vatican, and he and other members of Italy's Grand Council (its government) began plans to oust Mussolini. They eventually pushed Mussolini out of power and arrested him in July 1943, which was also when the Allied forces, led by the Americans, invaded

Italy through Sicily. Italy's new leader saw that defeat was imminent and negotiated a surrender with General Dwight D. Eisenhower. Italy eventually surrendered in September 1943.

But the Nazis, knowing that Italy was vulnerable after losses in both Greece and North Africa (where my grandfather Rocco served) and watching Mussolini oust his son-in-law from power, outlined a plan to invade Italy, which they escalated in mid-1943. Nazi troops moved down through Italy by September 1943, occupying most of the country and preparing for the Allied attacks. They also started scouting villages in the mountains of Abruzzo, including Cansano, hoping to build a defense line to stop the Allies. The defensive line, known as the Gustav Line, ran across Italy just several miles south of Cansano. The rugged mountainous terrain of central Italy, with its dense trees, rocky mountains, rivers, and ancient caves, was well-suited for a defense of the Allied attack.

At the same time, the Allies began escalating their plan for a two-front attack through Italy—the invasion through Sicily that started in July and a new front near Rome (known as the Battle of Anzio, which started in early 1944)—in what would become known as the Italian Campaign of World War II. The plan was simple—move through Italy from the south and push the Nazis out.

The fate of the Abruzzesi and Cansanesi was set. They were suddenly right in the middle of a hot spot of a tragic war that, thus far, had not really touched them. And, thanks to Mussolini's continued propaganda, they had no clue of what was about to hit them.

Between July and early September 1943, the new Italian regime hid Mussolini in mountain villages in Abruzzo, knowing that the Nazis would try to rescue him, as the Nazis saw value in a continued alliance with Mussolini. Eventually, the Italians took Mussolini to a remote mountain resort in Gran Sasso in the Apennine Mountains in northern Abruzzo, where he was rescued by Nazis in early September. With the support of the Nazis, Mussolini set up a puppet government in a northern region of Italy that was still under Nazi control. Mussolini took back control over the country's media and told all Italians that his son-in-law was a traitor and the cause of Italy's problems and that Italy was in control and would prevail in the war. The towns played his government news over loudspeakers. Sadly, and not knowing any better, many Cansanese and people elsewhere in Abruzzo believed it. They were unaware that troops were surrounding them from both the north and the south—Nazi troops from the north and Polish and American troops from the south.

Between September and early November 1943, the Nazis moved from town to town, identifying areas that they could occupy to battle the Allies. They initially came through Cansano several times without incident. Other towns were not so lucky. The Nazis' plan was to fortify their troops along the Gustav Line and the Sangro River, which was just north of the Gustav Line. To do this, they needed resources that they were lacking—slaves to dig trenches and mountain forts. Beginning in late September, they raided villages and captured civilian men, raped women and teenage girls, and forced the women and children to move into the mountains. The Cansanesi did not know this, and only knew of sporadic battles in Sulmona and to the south.

On October 11, 1943, two Nazis came to Cansano and met with the town mayor. They asked that the municipal building, post office, and a few of the larger Roman-style homes in the piazza be made available so that they could set up a permanent military installation in Cansano. Over the next few days, they also demanded that the civilians turn over all firearms and livestock. No one did, which angered the Nazis. It was about to get worse for the Cansanesi.

On the morning of October 17, 1943, the Nazis invaded Cansano. With a net of troops surrounding the town, the soldiers entered the piazza and began firing randomly in the streets. On a loudspeaker, which could be heard through the entire town, they demanded that all men ages sixteen to sixty report to the post office building; if they didn't, their home would be destroyed. No one turned themselves in and the Nazis carried out their promise. Men, fearing capture, tried to flee into the valley and the mountains but fell right into the Nazis' trap. Women and children hid in town and some escaped into the valley.

My father was seven. My mom was four.

During our 2014 visit to Cansano, my parents took me, Donato, and Izabella on a tour of *La Partayova*. We walked down the steep staircase, and my parents told us about each family that lived in the homes.

"Over here was a big oven that many families used to bake bread," Dad said, pointing to an abandoned home with no door. "And then, if you go down there, it was real scary," he said, pointing to a deep and narrow ravine next to the baker's home. "The Nazis came in and a lot of people went down here, including our family, and we were hiding. They could not find us."

His prior stories of the war were suddenly very real for me.

As the invasion continued on that fateful October morning, the Nazi soldiers ransacked many homes and eventually captured several military truckloads full of Cansanese men and teenage boys, whom they beat and enslaved, putting them to work making trenches to protect the Nazi soldiers from the Allies' bullets. "Somona bitches," Dad recalled.

Two of my grandfather Panfilo's brothers, Antonio and Rocco, were captured during this initial raid and held briefly in a camp a few miles from Cansano. They were somehow able to escape and return to the town, hiding in animal stalls to avoid recapture.

But unfortunately, something worse happened.

As we walked down the steep staircase during the 2014 visit, my dad stopped in front of a home and pointed to a window on the third story. "My cousin, who was twenty-one or twenty-two [at the time], was about to be captured and jumped out of the window. He hit his head on a rock and died."

Imagine that choice—be captured and enslaved or jump from the third story onto large rocks below and risk serious injury or death. My distant cousin chose death, or at least serious injury. The war I had heard and read so much about became more real for me that morning.

Over the next two weeks in late October 1943, the Nazis fortified their command in the piazza and continued looking for men, many of whom hid in their homes or in the valley and nearby mountains. Families began hiding possessions in the stables and small hidden rooms in their home. Furniture, wheat, corn, potatoes, clothing, money, and other important possessions were stored and hidden.

On November 1, 1943, the Nazi commander stationed in Cansano announced that all Cansanesi had to evacuate the town by noon on November 11. The Cansanesi were told that people who didn't voluntarily leave would be deported to Padua, a city in Northern Italy.

"We didn't know what to do or where we would go," my dad told me about that day during one of our morning walks.

Families were shocked and given ten days to determine what they would try to take with them—by foot or mule—into the rugged mountains, with winter cold and snow approaching.

Since many of the men had already either been captured or escaped into the hills to avoid capture, women and children were left to plan the departure. Some of the men, including my *nonni* (grandfathers) Rocco and Panfilo and some of their brothers, returned at night and helped their families plan and pack, escaping back to the mountains before dawn so the Nazis would not see them.

"Everyone—the whole town—was scared," my dad said. "Ah. *La paura* (the fear)," he remembered, shaking his head.

It was about to get worse, yet again.

On the morning November 11, 1943, as families packed their mules and belongings, the Nazis changed the plan and told the Cansanesi that each person could only take what he could carry.

"Can you imagine?" my dad told me about that morning during one of our walks in Cansano. "My mom, she was crying, '*Dio mio, che faremo.*' (My God, what will we do?)

The rest of their belongings, they were told, would become the property of the Nazis, including the homes, furniture, clothing, stored food, and animals. The Nazis also offered some people the opportunity to stay behind to become their servants and aids. A few did, and they were viewed as traitors, probably improperly, as they did what they thought was necessary to protect their families.

Life-altering—indeed, life-or-death—decisions had to be made.

CHAPTER FOURTEEN

The Stock Market

It is around seven o'clock on a cold morning in early January 2017. I am working out in my home gym in the basement. My dad called me many mornings before work. If we didn't talk in the morning, we would often talk on my drive home from the office. It was a comforting cadence. The subject of many of our morning talks was the stock market. By early 2000, my father had become a prolific trader. But he didn't have a computer—he religiously read the *Wall Street Journal* and watched the market shows on CNBC, Bloomberg, CNN, and Fox. His bedside credenza was filled with stock reports and materials he requested from the three to four brokers he worked with or directly from companies. He had a detailed system of reviewing the stock pages of the *Journal*, marking stocks that he liked based on dividends, earnings, market cap, and other statistics. He color coded them based on how much he liked them and circled them with a numbering system (one, two, or three) depending on if he would buy it then or keep watching it. He watched some stocks for many months before buying.

My phone rings. "Do you have any extra cash?" he starts.

"Umm, yes, some."

"Buy NRG Energy. It is down quite a bit the last few months and is trading around thirteen dollars a share. It is a good company, and I think it will go up to at least thirty dollars a share. I am buying \$50,000 to \$100,000."

"Wow, that is a lot." I wondered how dad had \$100,000 of cash available to put at risk.

"The market opens soon. Buy it now. It is going to go up."

"OK, I will."

I go back and finish my workout and forget to buy the stock.

Dad calls me on the way home from work. "Did you buy the stock?"

"No."

"You better. It is going to go up."

I bought the stock the next morning, and he was right. It traded at close to thirty dollars per share by the end of 2017. His best advice was about Target. He called on the morning of December 21, 2018.

"Juwaa, buy as much Target as you can. It is at sixty-one dollars a share and is going to go way up. It is a great stock and company. It is way undervalued."

"OK, I will."

Like NRG Energy, I didn't buy any that morning, but I did the next day. As I write this book in 2021, it is trading at over two hundred ten dollars a share.

Back to our January 2017 call.

"I am losing weight," he says. "I am down a few pounds. I am eating the same. I am always bloated and tired."

"That is strange. I am sure it is nothing, Dad. Maybe try to eat better. More vegetables and less meat and cheese. I feel a lot better since going on a plant-based diet."

"I don't eat a lot of those things."

"I think it is normal to lose weight as you get older. Get some exercise. That will help your energy."

"How is that big construction case you are working?"

"Pretty good. We go to trial soon."

"Are you on the right side of the case?"

"Yes, Dad." He always asked that question about my cases or deals.

"Well, I hope you beat the heck out of them. Go home and have a nice dinner, some wine, and get some rest."

"I will. I will talk to you tomorrow. Good night."

"Good night."

CHAPTER FIFTEEN

Chiacchierone

When we arrive at my cousin Rocco's bed-and-breakfast after our early-morning walk around town that day in June 2013, my Zio Pietro is just returning from tending to the sheep at his ranch, a morning routine for him. Most mornings, Zio and Rocco made fresh pecorino cheese or sheep ricotta, which Pietro's ranch was known for. He sold the cheese and ricotta, as well as lamb meat, to local markets and restaurants in the neighboring towns, and he insisted on delivering his products himself.

"*Hai gia fatto un giro del paese,*" my uncle asks. "Did you do a walk around the town?"

"*Sì, Zio,*" I said. "*Io amo questo paese.*" "Yes, Uncle. I love this town."

"*Sei andato alla Partayova*?" he asks. "Did you go to *La Partayova*?"

I nod yes. "*È triste quello che è successo lì.* (It is sad what happened there)."

"*Nipote, il paese è morto, e le case si stanno deteriorando,*" he responds. "*Nessuno vive qui caro nipote. paccato.* (Nephew, the town is dead and the homes are deteriorating. No one lives here. It is a shame)."

"*La Guerra,*" he continues. "*Una miseria che non può essera compresa.* (The war. A misery that cannot be comprehended)."

The words hang in the air.

"*Fra, hai già lavorato*?" my dad asks his brother. "*Lavori troppo.* (Brother, you have already been working? You work too hard)."

"Fra, c'è del lavoro da fare e nessuno per farlo," he responds. "Brother, there is work to do and no one to do it."

This was a common exchange between them. My dad wanted his older brother to enjoy the fruits of retirement, and my uncle was a bit irritated that his younger brother was telling him what to do.

My uncle enunciates each word with passion and emphasis, but slowly, perhaps wanting me to understand him.

And, unlike all of the Italian I had heard from other Cansanesi growing up and what I heard on all of my trips to Italy, he enunciates the last vowel in each word with emphasis. It was common in Cansano to cut off the end of almost every word, and their own dialect had developed over decades. So, I listen to him with interest, and the language is beautiful.

As a freshman at the University of Colorado in 1985, I had to take three years of a foreign language, so I signed up for Italian. Piece of cake, I thought. I grew up around the language—indeed, it was my first language. And even though I didn't use it frequently—only a bit with my grandmothers when they were alive—how hard could this be? I quickly learned that the Italian I grew up around was very different from the proper Italian taught in school. And worse, I discovered that my family and the other Cansanesi had made up words, combining English and Italian words. And most sentences that my parents spoke at home were a combination of English and Italian. For example, once when I was counting the cash while closing up the grocery store my parents owned when I was a teenager, my father said: *"Juwaa, quand si finit* with the register, *driva* the *carra* and take your mom *alla casa. Vado ai cani."*

What he meant to say was "Giovanni, when you are done with the cash registers, drive the car and take your mom home. I am going to the dog track." *"Driva"* was a made-up word for drive, and *"carra"* was made up for car, and most of the words were not fully enunciated. But, to my teenaged ear, this was correct. I really had no idea it was wrong until I was called on in class my freshman year of college and asked to say, "Drive the car." The proper way is *"Guida la macchina."* I said, *"Driva la carra."* The professor looked at me like I was crazy and maybe joking or mocking her. I wasn't.

My three years of Italian proved to be some of my hardest courses at the University of Colorado, especially my final two years with Pamela Marcantonio, whose husband, ironically enough, was also Cansanese.

In Cansano that June 2013 morning, a few locals and other Cansanesi from New York and Canada who are visiting their birthplace come out of their homes to greet my father as he chats with my uncle. He hasn't seen a few of them for decades. They immediately exchange what is known as *il bacetto*, the famous Italian greetings. Greetings in Italy are nothing like the ones we practice in the United States, but they are sometimes awkward if not performed correctly. Friends and acquaintances, both men and women, exchange air kisses—*il bacetto*—on both cheeks. I wasn't prepared for this and was surprised the day before when we first arrived and my uncle and cousins reached out to greet me with *il bacetto*. An awkward dance ensued. Do I actually kiss their cheeks? I learned the answer is no, unless you are very close friends or family. And which way do you start, on your right or left? After bonking noses and foreheads a few times, I learned that most people start on their left (although you have to approach it carefully and take the cue from the other person). But even if you don't actually kiss the other person's cheek, you lightly touch your cheek to theirs. I was startled by the rough beards of my uncle and cousin the day before. This was going to take some getting used to—and some practice.

With his fingers in the shape of a tulip, my uncle raises his right hand and says to my dad, *"E, signor chiacchierone, dobbiamo andare.* (Hey, Mr. Talker, we need to get going)."

"Tuo padre è un chiacchierone," my Zio Pietro says to me. "Your father is a *chiacchierone*."

Chiacchierone was a word I had never heard before, but I instantly liked the sound of it.

"*Che cosa significa 'chiacchierone'*?" I ask Zio. "What does chiacchierone mean?"

"Someone who loves to talk," he explains in Italian.

For the rest of that trip and for years to come, I teasingly called my father a *chiacchierone*, which always brought a smile to his face.

CHAPTER SIXTEEN

Polenta and Dandelions

In early November 1943, all Cansanesi faced being viewed as traitors for staying and serving the Nazis, being sent to a prisoner of war camp if they refused to leave, or moving into the mountains surrounding the town as the harsh winter approached. My family chose freedom. "My dad said no way we help the Nazis," my mom told me about the decision. She tells me this story often, and it was the type of courage that I didn't comprehend. "Our neighbors, they stayed and helped the Nazis. Not us. No way."

My dad's family—his mother Filomena; his father Rocco, who had just returned from fighting for the Italian army in Libya; my dad's two older brothers, Armando and Pietro; his one-year-old brother Luciano; and my dad, together with several other Ruscittis—left the town by foot on the morning of November 11, 1943, and set up camp in the nearby mountains. It was a cold morning, and they walked on foot a few miles, down the valley and up the mountain to a location where they could build a temporary shelter. They constructed a large tent from tree branches, weeds, and plants. "That is where we went to hide," my dad says during our walk the second morning of our stay in Cansano. I look in the distance to the densely packed mountainside, unable to imagine what it must have been like for my then-seven-year-old father. "I can't believe what we went through," he says.

My mom's family—her father; her two uncles, Antonio and Rocco; my grandmother Nunziata and her father, Donato D'Orazio; my great-grandmother Angela Morelli DiGiallonardo; my mom's infant sister Liberta; my mom; and a few other DiGiallonardo family members—did the same thing, setting up in an area known as *La Refenza*.

"The men built something like a teepee," my mom told me later.

"It was very cold and we had nothing to eat or drink except the few things we packed."

"We had nothing to eat," my dad often told me.

"We ate dandelions and polenta. Polenta for breakfast, lunch, and dinner. Can you imagine that? No salt, no oil. No pepper."

I heard this story often, almost the same words each time. Polenta is an easy, cheap dish made with cornmeal. A meal for peasants.

"When we was forced to leave on the eleventh of November, we took what food we could. Some cornmeal, some flour, some dried figs, some cheese, dried sausage. We didn't know how long we would be gone," Dad told me during our 2014 trip to Cansano, as we walked up the road toward the train station above the town.

"But we didn't have a lot and the Nazis had already taken many of our things in October. We ate polenta every day."

As with most Italian immigrant families, Sunday dinner was a big event when I was a child. My mom would make some of my favorite meals—lasagna; ravioli; a very thin two-layered pizza with salt, black pepper, and olive oil on top and garlic, red pepper, and white anchovies in between the two layers (to-die-for good); and spaghetti—all using homemade items, from the pasta to the dough for the pizza and bread to the sauce to the sausage. And one of my favorites was polenta, in part for the taste and in part of the production. This was not your ordinary polenta.

My mom made a large saucepan of polenta (enough to feed at least twenty people), and my dad would take the polenta and spread it over the entire kitchen table. On half of the polenta, he put red sauce and pieces of sausage cooked in the sauce. On the other half, he sprinkled olive oil and sausage. He would finish it off with a healthy dose of a mix of parmesan and pecorino Romano cheese. The family would sit around the table and eat the polenta. Sometimes my aunts, uncles, and cousins would come by. On the side was veal, lamb, or goat that was cooked in the sauce. My favorite was the olive oil polenta. So simple but simply amazing.

Fast-forward to a more recent memory: Aggie and I took my parents on many trips between 2013 and 2019, and we took them to many restaurants for special occasions. My dad was quick to complain about the price of everything—from airline tickets to hotels to restaurant prices. It was the nature of being raised in a condition of scarcity. He would ask me how much everything I bought cost. To protect him—and to avoid his lecturing me—I learned to give my dad what I call the "parent price." The parent price was always at least 50 percent less than the real price, sometimes 75 percent less. "Juwaa, that is too much," he would say of the parent price of almost everything and anything I purchased or spent on our trips.

But I learned to quickly shut down his complaints by saying, "Dad, if you complain one more time about how much this is costing, you are paying for it."

He would chuckle and say, "OK, Mr. Bigga Shot lawyer. I won't say a word."

Until the next trip, of course, when the exact same conversation took place.

For my mom's birthday in 2016, we took them to a restaurant in Boulder. On the menu was a dandelion salad and a polenta dish with lamb. I pointed it out to him, "Look, Dad, dandelions and polenta."

"Can you imagine that? That was all we had to eat in the old country," he responded, shaking his head in disbelief at the irony.

"And now it is a delicacy," I responded.

"Can you believe the prices? Fifteen dollars for a dandelion salad and twenty-five dollars for polenta? *Mannaggia la miseria.* I can buy enough polenta at the store to feed a family of six for the month," he said in disgust.

"*Mannaggia la miseria*" means damn the misery. It was one of my father's favorite expressions.

"Dad, do you want to pay for dinner?"

"OK, OK. I will shut up," he said laughing.

And so it went.

CHAPTER SEVENTEEN

The Harmonica Album

I *way* overplanned for our 2013 trip, creating undue stress for myself and the family if we were behind my schedule. Our itinerary included five days in Cansano, four days in Rome, and five days on the Amalfi coast, sandwiched between two travel days. I wanted to see so many things and go to all the places I had been hearing of. But I forgot one important thing—we needed down time to relax, especially during the Cansano portion so that we could enjoy the magical town. The need to slow down and enjoy the pace of life in Cansano, among other things, led to me booking all my subsequent trips back, including trips in 2014, 2017, and 2019.

On the agenda for the second day in Cansano was renting a car in Sulmona so that we could visit some nearby towns. My plan was to do day trips to Campo di Giove, Pacentro, Pescocostanzo, Pescara, and Sulmona.

At my parents' insistence, all of my scheduling for this portion of the trip had to center around two events—the *La Festa di San Giovanni* on June 24 and the market in Sulmona on Wednesday the twenty-sixth. On June 24, Cansano, like all towns in Italy, celebrates San Giovanni, or Saint John, the patron saint of the town and many others in Italy. It starts with a mid-morning religious procession from the church, through the town and piazza, and ending back at the church with a service. Then a large celebration is held that night with live music and local delicacies, including grilled lamb kabobs in the piazza.

"You need to see the celebration of San Giovanni," my mom insisted while we were planning. "That was one of the best days of the year when we were young. The music, the food. Dancing. People were happy."

And she would throw in, with emphasis, "And you are named *Giovanni*, so we must see it."

Beginning this trip, I discovered that summer and fall festivals, especially in small towns like Cansano, are an important part of the Italian culture. Many Italian festivals, like San Giovanni, are religious, as many towns have a patron saint they celebrate. Others are based on historical events. And yet others, like *La Festa di Agnello* (the festival of the lamb, held in Cansano each August), are just for getting together. Italians love to come together to see, be seen, eat, drink, sing, dance, and celebrate life. *La dolce vita*. The sweet life. The festivals include exhibitions, pilgrimages, processions with people dressed in period costume, live music and dancing, contests between neighborhoods of the town, flag-throwers, amazing local foods and wine, and fireworks.

For my dad, it was all about the market.

"We need to go to the market in Sulmona on Wednesday," my dad reminded me as we planned the trip. "You will love it."

My uncle said that he had arranged for the rental car in Sulmona, but he had to make deliveries of his fresh ricotta and lamb to the local restaurants and markets in the neighboring towns, so the rental car would have to wait. My cousin Rocco offered to take us to Campo di Giove, which was a few miles away. But I was very excited to show Aggie, Donato, and Izabella *La Partayova*, which had profoundly touched me that morning. So we decided to do Campo di Giove that afternoon.

My dad, *cugino* (cousin) Rocco, and the four of us walk down *Via Roma* to *Via Oriente*, a charming street that I visited often on my trips. *Via Oriente* is about 100 yards long and ends with an alley to the left and a steep and winding/jagged staircase to the right, with numerous homes tucked into each possible area. The homes are a mixture of rocks and limestone, some new, some old, some white, some yellow, and some pink, with balconies hanging over many of the windows and second story doors. We walk down the staircase, and sidewalks emerge in each direction, with more homes built along the mountain landscape. The sounds of family life can be heard from some of the homes. A young boy tells his mom he is ready for *pranzo*, or lunch.

At the end of one sidewalk that flanked to the right is an arched tunnel that frames a magnificent view of the dense and lush valley below. A small creek is visible in the bottom of the valley. "We would walk the animals to the creek for water and pasture," my dad says, pointing to the bottom. Donato takes a picture—one of my favorite photos—of me and Izabella looking down the valley.

We continue walking down, and the homes all begin to look abandoned. The homes are old, made mostly of rock. We turn to our left, and a row of what used to be three-story homes is to our right and in front of us. The roofs and walls of many of the homes are caved in, making some homes look like they were destroyed by bombs. Izabella asks my father if the buildings were destroyed by bombs during World War II.

"No, there were no bombs here."

"Then what happened, Grandpa?"

"People had to leave after the war. There were no jobs, no food. No nothing." And then he added, "People wanted a better life. The people left and no one takes care of these houses. So, they just started falling apart."

He went on. "The war was misery. After the war was worse. We had nothing. You know what we ate as a luxury meal, *pani duru*."

Pani duru is a simple dish that is made by soaking old crusty bread in boiling water, removing it, and seasoning the now wet mushy bread with olive oil, salt, and pepper. I had seen my parents eat this many times in my childhood, not knowing its origin.

He continues, "Until the early '50s, and then things got a little bit better."

We remain quiet, thinking about what he had just said.

"But, Grandpa, we made the most of it. We enjoyed each other. The simple life. Not like today. Singing, playing music, being with the family and friends," he says to Izabella.

My mom and dad had a strange way of talking to their grandchildren—my mom called them "grandma" and my dad called them "grandpa."

A memory surfaces. "Juwaa, get me my harmonica," my dad told the younger me, sipping his homemade red wine. After a few glasses of wine, my dad loved playing the harmonica for us and my mom, and he played it beautifully. Whether it was just us or when family or friends visited, he loved playing the harmonica, especially Sunday afternoons—songs like *Il Cacciatore Nel Bosco*, *Santa Lucia*, *Al di Là*, *La Domenica Andando Alla Messa*, *La Canzone Degli Immigrati*, or his favorite, *La Campagnola*. In my memory, I was about seven years old, and we had visitors from out of town, all Cansanesi. Italians are never shy with sharing their way of life. They sat around the kitchen table for hours, drinking wine and my dad playing the harmonica. There was singing and laughter. I think about my dad's words about the simple life and community and making the most of it. I rarely slowed down for such simple things. Too busy building my practice. Too busy coaching Little League sports. Just too busy to really slow down and enjoy the simple things and the company of family and friends. This would change.

Years after this first trip to Cansano, Donato and Dante recorded and then published my dad playing the harmonica. *The Harmonica Album*, released in 2020, is a mixture of my dad playing the harmonica and telling stories with mom about their childhood.

"Grandpa, you will maka milliona dollars if'a you record music like this," Dad tells Donato, the family musician, in his thick Italian accent.

"OK, Grandpa," Donato responds.

"I love music," Dad says at the end of the album. "And whatever I play is all by ear."

He continues. "I never forget at my age, I never forget my younger age when a bunch of friends, boys, girls, we get together, sometimes by group, girls or boys. And we, we used to love to play. We were good accordion players. One of the guys became a professor."

On the album, his voice is aged and the tempo is slow.

"He became one of the top professors of music in Italy. Those people, they are all dead now. I am still alive, thank God."

The last few years before this recording had been hard on him.

"And that is all I can tell you today. I want to thank all of you for listening to me, and I hope you enjoyed that. Again, thank you very, very much. Again, I am Emiliano Ruscitti and thank you very much for listening to me. OK, bye. *Ciao*."

The album ends. A bucket list item satisfied.

^ ^ ^ ^ ^

We continue our walk. We turn to our left to walk down another sidewalk or *via*, and many of the homes have steep staircases, now crumbling and falling apart, leading up to the doors. The homes were built on a side of a steep mountain, so many of the homes were constructed wherever there was available land within the town (people wanted to stay within the town for safety, so no homes were built outside of this tight area), resulting with homes of different materials, shapes, and sizes literally stacked on each other. The resulting architecture was stunning, even with the homes in a state of decay. This short street led to *Via Due Porte* and became one of my favorites; several of the wood doors that hung from the arched entries over perched balconies were a display of magnificent colors—blues, greens, yellows, and pinks—that had peeled away and/or were exposed to the elements over years, revealing a colorful masterpiece of abstract painting.

We turn to our right and walk down *Via Due Porte* toward *La Partayova*, going the opposite direction my father and I had traveled that morning. A fork in the sidewalk appears on the right.

"Up there is the church your mom and I got married in," Dad says to me. "The earthquake in 2009 about almost destroyed it. We will see if we can get in."

"And this building on the right is an old castle," he says of a massive building that overlooked the valley to the right and the valley to Sulmona and formed the highest point in town. "It belonged to the rich barons that controlled the town over a thousand years ago."

"Can we go into it?" Donato asks.

"I don't know. We will come back when we have more time to see the church and castle."

I ask why the town leaders have not restored the church and castle.

"Juwaa, who knows. No money. *E nessuno abita qui.* (No one lives here)."

We walk down into *La Partayova*, and Dad tells Donato and Izabella many of the same stories he had told me earlier that morning and over the years. They listened intently.

"Zio, dovremmo tornare a case. Il pranzo è pronto," Rocco says. "Uncle, we should return to the house. Lunch is ready."

"Va bene," my dad says.

"Va bene," "allora," and *"buongiorno"* are phrases you hear all day long in Italy, no matter where you are. *Va bene* means "all right" or "sounds good." *Allora* is a versatile word that means something like "so," "well then," or "OK then" and is a great filler word in conversation. And, of course, *buongiorno* is "hello." Italians love saying *buongiorno* to each other and perfect strangers they pass on the street. While it technically means "good morning," Italians use it all day long and up until evening, when it switches to *"buona sera,"* or "good evening."

After an early simple but delicious lunch of mortadella (a large Italian baloney with pieces of pistachios in the meat), prosciutto, fresh cheese, bread, and a salad, we drive up to Campo di Giove.

"We need to go soon and before the shops close," my cousin says in Italian.

What he says doesn't register, yet. It was a Sunday, so I assumed everything was open all day.

"I hope I see my *compare*," my dad says as we drive up. *"Compare"* is Italian for godfather. "He lives here and I haven't seen him since we were here in 1986."

The road twists and turns, and we get a great view of my Zio Pietro's ranch on the right and then, a bit further up, a magnificent view of Cansano down below. The steepness of the mountain that the town sits on is pronounced, and the town disappears as it blends seamlessly into the valley heading toward Sulmona.

Pointing to an area on the right that is covered with dense trees and bushes, he says, "We used to take our sheep to a pasture back there. Sometimes, we would sleep there. Our parents knew we were safe. Except for the damn wild pigs. They were mean and sometimes they kept us awake all night."

"How old were you?" I ask.

"Twelve, thirteen. Something like that."

Campo di Giove reminds me of small Colorado ski towns, with a mix of newer condominiums and older homes like those in Cansano. Campo di Giove has a rich history, dating back to at least the Roman Empire. The older homes are like those in Cansano but with more local rock and less limestone. Fewer homes are abandoned here and the town looks more prosperous.

We park the car to walk some of the streets. This part of town is built on the mountainside, and a complex web of sidewalks connects the two- and three-story homes in an intricate maze. Most of the main entrances to the homes are elevated, with short staircases leading to the doors. Some sidewalks are straight, some are curved, all are steep and well-maintained. Colorful flowerpots adorn rustic rails that frame many of the windows and staircases to the main entries. Each home has stunning dark wood doors and windows. The sounds of life emanate from the homes, and I feel like an intruder. A few small piazzas appear during our walk, a place for the neighbors in each small neighborhood to commune.

We walk down a stunningly long, steep staircase made from white marble, which is very different from the rest of the area. I wonder what life was like here in the '40s and '50s.

The town's large piazza appears on the left and is buzzing with activity. In the distance, a group of six boys dribbles a soccer ball. Ranging in age between five and eight, the boys are very skilled. Behind them is a magnificent home, now a museum, that is hundreds of years old and once belonged to the town baron. Several cafés and gelato shops surround the piazza. The Maiella mountains race up into the sky in the background, casting an imposing shadow over the town.

It is about twelve-thirty p.m., and another Italian tradition called *riposo*, which I knew nothing about, is about to happen. Some people are sipping coffees, while others are drinking beer or wine. Some are having gelato. Classic Italian music is playing in the background from the coffee shop. While everyone is engaged in a different activity, they are all doing the same thing—talking with each other.

We walk to the *gelateria* and have a small gelato. "Wow, I have never had a gelato this good," Izabella says. And she is right—at least for now. We repeated this phrase over and over each time we had gelato in different towns. And we said the same thing with each meal we had—the food tasted better here for some reason. Clean and simple, with deep and rich flavors. Over the next few years, we discovered Michelin-star restaurants hidden in the smallest villages throughout Italy, each serving food we had never tasted in the United States.

My dad starts to laugh loudly and says, *"Dio mio! Caro compare! Come stai!"*

"My god! Dear godfather, how are you?"

Dad rushes toward an older gentleman who is talking with a group of men around the fountain in the center of the piazza. They embrace, laugh, cry, and reminisce for almost an hour, as the rest of us walk around the center of town. The shops and restaurants begin to close.

"Cugino, che cosa sta succedendo?" I ask Rocco. *"Perch è tutto sta chiudendo?"*

"Cousin, what is going on? Why is everything closing?"

"In Italia, facciamo qualcosa chiamato riposo," he responds. *"Tutti i negozi chiudono, la gente torna a case a fa un grande pranzo con vino, si riposa e poi torna al lavoro più tardi nel pomeriggio."*

"In Italy, all of the businesses close, people go home and have a big lunch with some wine, and then they rest; then they go back to work later in the afternoon."

"Every day, even on weekends?" I ask in Italian.

"Sì, è un' usanza importante," he says. "Yes, it is an important social custom."

"And during the workweek?" I ask in Italian, flabbergasted.

"Si," he says emphatically and with some curiosity as to why I was struggling with the concept.

Wow, I think to myself. That would never happen in the United States. I was a bit annoyed, though, as this impacted my vacation and plans. Silly, right? Later in this trip and in years to come, I learned to love this time of day and wished we had the same custom back home.

"Chiacchierone, hai finito," I tease my dad, excited to be able to use my new favorite Italian word. "Mr. Talker, are you done?"

He embraces his godfather and they say goodbye. We return to Cansano for some rest. Aggie, the kids, and my parents take a nap. Not a napper, I walk the town. No one is out but me.

They take this *riposo* custom seriously, I think to myself. I should learn to do this.

I walk down to the piazza and instead of turning right toward *La Partayova*, I turn left and walk through the piazza to *Via Don Francesco de Bartolomeis*, the road that leads to Pescocostanzo. A soccer pitch is on the right, and I continue walking a quarter mile until I reach the old cemetery on the left. I see a tiny church named *La Chiesa di San Donato* across the road from the cemetery. I walk up to the church and try to open the door. The church is locked and apparently has not been used in years. It was large enough for maybe ten people. I wonder why they built such a small church and why it was no longer used.

The Maiella mountains tower over and envelop the town like a curtain. The arched bridge I had seen that morning is in front of me in the distance, and I see some twisting roads on the left high above the town. I stop and take in the view. A sense of peace and serenity overtakes me.

A walking meditation.

The worries of back home and client projects and deadlines are long gone.

CHAPTER EIGHTEEN

Rina

My sister Rina, who is six years older than I, was diagnosed with stage III, noninvasive breast cancer on November 16, 2016, and had been undergoing chemotherapy for several months. She was getting worse and the doctors were concerned that it was something called inflammatory breast cancer, a rare and dangerous version of the disease. In early April 2017, I talked to my dad on our daily call.

"Do you think she is going to be okay?" he asked.

I don't have a good feeling about her condition, but I don't want to worry him or my mom, so I lie. "I think so, Dad. But the doctors are concerned it is a different type of breast cancer. I am trying to get her in to MD Anderson in Houston. It is the best in the country for certain types of cancer."

"Please do what you can to get her in."

"I am doing everything I can. How are you feeling?"

"I am down a few more pounds, and I am always tired."

My father was not a victim and never complained. And he was the most energetic eighty-one-year-old I knew, with each day filled with different activities—bocce, playing cards, working in his shop, entertaining friends, and shopping with my mom. He had been telling me about his slowly declining weight and lack of energy since early January, and I was starting to get worried.

"Dad, I think you need to get this checked out. Make an appointment right away."

"I will, Juwaa. I hate those damn doctors. They will find something wrong with me."

"I am sure it will be fine, but get it checked out."

"OK. Get your sister into Houston, OK?"

"I will."

CHAPTER NINETEEN

Kicked Out of Their Homes

I wake up early on our second morning in Cansano and quietly exit our room. It is San Giovanni's Day—June 24, 2013—and my first chance to be part of an Italian festival. I am looking forward to another predawn walk around the town after a night filled with a large multicourse meal and lots of wine. My cousin has set aside the entire bed and breakfast for our visit, and Aggie and I have the upstairs suite. Donato and Izabella share the other upstairs suite, and my parents are in a downstairs suite. The building—which had been rebuilt sometime in the last fifteen years on a property belonging to a distant relative and that the Nazis occupied during the 1943 invasion—was relatively modern, yet it maintained the architecture of this part of the town. As I walk down the staircase in the white outdoor foyer and step onto the pink cobblestone, the distinctive smell of the old village overtakes me immediately. Gentle waves of leaves on the century-old trees ripple in the light breeze that blows down *Via Roma*. Even in mid-June, the morning mountain air is cool, and the combination of the pinyon-like scents of the local pine burning in fireplaces and the sweet and oaky smell of indigenous plants and bushes in the valley across the street creates a distinctive fragrance that engulfs me—a fragrance that I would never forget. Mixed in is a musky smell from the old limestone and rock buildings. I look across the street and notice the lights on the old cast-iron light poles, slightly yellow in color. A comforting chill runs down my body, and I feel the presence of an almost spiritual source that would bring me back to this town over and over in the coming years.

I walk down *Via Roma* for about fifty yards until the street forks into two paths—*Via Casale* in front of me and *Via Oriente* to my right. I am drawn to *Via Oriente*, which I had walked the day before. The street, which is more like an alleyway, is very narrow and in some places is only five to six feet wide. Tightly packed homes line both sides of the street. Some are remodeled and occupied, and some are dilapidated and were abandoned decades ago. I notice a yellow limestone building to my left, and directly in front of me about twenty yards ahead is a pinkish limestone building. Both had been recently remodeled and the walls look like stucco. Other buildings were remodeled with rocks from the valley to match the architecture of old. On the right, the houses overlook the deep ravine.

The street widens, and some cars are parked along the way. I turn down a short alley on the left that connects back to *Via Casale*, and on my left, I see my dad standing in front of the bed and breakfast. I walk back.

"*Buongiorno*," he says. "You are up early again."

"Yes, I love the mornings here."

"*Un caffè*?" he asks. "A coffee?"

"Yes."

We walk down to the main dining area and make an espresso like we did the day before, which we enjoy with some Italian pastries. My uncle had picked up some pastries at a *pasticceria* (pasty shop) in Sulmona, including some gluten-free cookies for me. Yes, I am an Italian with a severe gluten and casein (the protein found in dairy) intolerance. I have had stomach issues my whole life and was routinely, and incorrectly, diagnosed with one ailment after another over the years, including a concern in my thirties that I had stomach cancer. I didn't, and it wasn't until Aggie read a nutrition book that she connected the dots and suggested I might have a gluten allergy. Like with most things, she was right. We changed what we ate, which was very hard for me, as I ate cheese with literally every meal. Aggie discovered her true calling with nutrition. She became a certified integrative health coach, treating the causes of health issues and not the symptoms. When planning the trip, I was very concerned that I would not be able to eat gluten-free and would be sick the entire trip. And how would I explain to my uncle that I couldn't eat pasta and bread, the staples of an Italian diet? It seemed like a silly kind of "disease" that was only recently dreamed up in America to diagnose undiagnosable stomach issues caused by decades of poor diets and eating genetically modified foods. I learned how to say the following things in Italian: "Do you have a gluten-free menu?", "I am allergic to gluten.", and "Do you have gluten-free bread and pasta?"

To my surprise, Italy, like most European countries, had long known and understood that many people have celiac disease or have some intolerance to gluten. Every restaurant had gluten-free options (including pasta and bread, which, in 2013, was still not the case back home); grocery stores had sections devoted to gluten-free products (something that was not yet common in the United States); you could buy many gluten-free products in pharmacies; and, as it turns out, my uncle grew a crop of gluten-free grains that he sold for making gluten-free pastas and breads. So, while I stayed away from gluten during this and all of our subsequent trips to Italy, I occasionally ate the local cheeses and, to my surprise, never got sick. Perhaps it was because GMOs are outlawed in Italy and the cheese was purer. Or maybe, like my dad used to say, it is just because everything is better in Italy.

We finish our coffee and pastries, and without a plan, we walk across the street toward my mom's childhood home and walk up the road toward my uncle's ranch. Dad points across the valley to a distant mountain.

"That is where we hid when the Nazis kicked us out in 1943. We stayed in the mountains for about a month, until a big snow came," my father says.

"No food, no water, nothing. Everyone was sick and *magro* (skinny)."

I listen but don't say anything.

"My dad knew a lady in Sulmona. She had a big house, and he hoped she would let us stay there. We took everything we had, which was nothing." He says the word "nothing" with emphasis.

"We walked the twelve kilometers in the snow. It snowed one to three feet of snow. We were wet and had no protection. I was just a little kid."

I continue to listen, but I later regretted not asking more questions.

"Many of the poor people had nowhere to go," Dad recalled. "They stayed in the mountains for months. Some of the men got captured. Some people starved. People were always on the lookout for the Nazis, who were going through the mountains to try to find the men and teenage boys to make them work and build trenches. And some were really no good. They find the young girls and abuse them. Dirty sons of bitches."

As my father talks, a memory emerges. It was a story I had heard from my mom numerous times, and I was now gaining perspective. She and her family were stuck in the mountains as well, but fortunately they were able to move to an old, abandoned farmhouse in an area close to Sulmona my mom called *La Casetta* when the December 1943 snowstorm hit. She told my boys the story in 2018, the same way I had heard it numerous times. They documented it:

> One time, my grandma Angela wanted to go see if she could find some food. I went with her. I was a little girl maybe five years old. So, we was walking and the Nazis stop us and they start talking to us, asking where we were staying and where the men were. My grandma Angela would not answer. So, they start to hit my grandma, and they broke her collarbone. Because I was a little girl, they wanted to give me candy. I didn't want it. I was mad. Can you imagine? They hurt my grandma but give me candy? No way. I was very scared, and I got blisters all over my head and lost all of my hair because I was scared. I had to wear a hat for a long time until it grew back.

I think about that story as my dad continues his.

"Some of the people who stayed in the mountains, they tried to sneak back into town for shelter that winter. They looked for food they had stored. But the Nazis had taken almost everything. A few lucky families, including some of my mom's *parenti*, or relatives, the DiGiacomo family, my grandmother Anastasia's cousins, were able to sneak back in, and they stayed in some of the old homes in *La Partayova*. The Nazis didn't go to the area much."

"Where did you stay?" I ask.

"Well, after living in the mountains for a few months, we walked to Sulmona during the storm in the middle of the night to avoid the Nazis. It took several hours, but we made it. Thank God for that old lady. Her name was Cruscificia. My brother says that she is still alive. I would love to go see her," he says.

I didn't agree, but instead I remained silent—one of my life's biggest regrets. During our 2014 return trip, my dad again mentioned that he wanted to see the old lady that saved his family during World War II, but I was unable to take him before we had to return home. Fortunately, my parents stayed a few weeks longer than we did and were able to go see her. She remembered him.

"*O figlio mio. Sono così felice che tu sia venuto a trovarmi*," she said when he introduced himself. "Oh, my son. I am so happy that you came to see me."

When Dad saw her in 2014, Cruscificia was well over one hundred years old—an old lady. She was in her thirties when she took in my father's family in the 1940s, but she probably felt old to my dad then—he was only seven.

CHAPTER TWENTY

Survival

Giulio DiGiacomo, my father's second or third cousin, was ten years old during the Nazi occupation of Cansano and wrote a harrowing book titled *Survival* about his family's experience in the mountains in late 1943 and their successful entry back into Nazi-occupied Cansano in early 1944. I read the book in 2020 and was brought back in time to my dad's stories about the events of 1943 and 1944 in passages such as this one:

> "That experience bonded us forever because it involved acts of unquestionable altruism and compassion, which reveals the true soul of a being. Pain and suffering is shared among the afflicted. There is no other way! It is human nature, the instinct in us that takes over and prevails. The behavior that was appropriate in the course of normal life is overridden, supplanted by the rule of the forest: that of survival."

Some more World War II history. The Nazis occupied Cansano from November 11, 1943, to May 18, 1944. During that time, the Allies, who had invaded Italy in the summer of 1943 through Sicily, had been slowly pushing the Nazi forces back, liberating town by town. The Allies eventually freed Cansano in May 1944 after a final battle on May 18, 1944.

The Nazis' main defense line, the Gustav Line, ran just south of Cansano across the entire Italian peninsula and blocked the entry to Rome. The Allies' strategy was to take Rome by cracking the Gustav Line from the south and then securing the beachhead near the coastal town of Anzio, about thirty-eight miles south of Rome. The southern attack through Sicily was slow, as the Allied forces were met with strong Nazi resistance and treacherous winter conditions in the mountains of central and southern Italy.

The Battle of Anzio took place from January 22, 1944, to June 5, 1944, ending with the Allies' successful capture of Rome. It started with the Allied amphibious landing known as Operation Shingle. By midnight, 36,000 soldiers—including Aggie's Great Uncle Delbert James Powers—and 3,200 vehicles had landed on the beaches. The hope was that the attack would force the Nazis to shift some of their resources from the center of the Gustav Line—the town of Cassino and the mountains behind it—to Anzio, thereby weakening both lines.

The plan worked but took six months of deadly battles and the loss of thousands of civilian lives to execute. The Nazis knew that by hiding out in small towns, the Allies would have a difficult time finding them and would be forced to make tough military decisions—trying to execute pinpoint aerial attacks in the middle of occupied towns. This meant that civilians would be endangered. This also meant having to rely on dated military intelligence to locate the Nazis. As they did in Cansano, the Nazis placed military commands near piazzas and churches to make their discovery very difficult for the Allies.

I remember at five years of age watching Walter Cronkite on *CBS Evening News* with my dad, Cronkite's somber, slow-paced voice talking about the Vietnam War and a deadly attack that left many innocent civilians dead. The images shown were horrific to the young child version of me.

"The same things happened to us in World War II," my dad interjected. "The Nazis killed many innocent people and then the Americans and British did the same thing. No one was good."

And then he recalled, "They dug a big hole and they put the poor dead people in the hole, piled on top of each other like cord wood. *Disgraziati.*" A *disgraziato* is a rotten or wretched person.

In 2018, my father shared with Dante the following:

> When Germany came in, the Nazi soldiers, you know what they was doing? They tried to get all the people to put them to work making trenches to protect themselves from the bullets. They killed many innocent people. And then the Americans came in to find the Nazis. The Nazis, they were hiding far away, somewhere else. You know where the Americans go bomb? The piazza, the church, the hospital. Innocent people died. Why they wanna kill innocent people?

And that was the story of war, especially in the Nazi-occupied towns of Abruzzo between 1943 and 1944.

My father had a deep disdain for war and a distrust of politicians and the media. "War is only for the politicians, and they control the media," he would say. "They tell you only what they want you to know. Sons of bitches."

Propaganda was key to politics and governing in World War II and in the years that followed. There was no internet, no cable TV, no social media, and no fact-checking. In the United States at the time, there were a few TV stations and the print media. And many were controlled by politicians, much like today. My father was leery of what he heard and read.

"Juwaa, believe half of what you see and none of what you hear," he told me often when I was growing up.

"What is he talking about? He is crazy," I would think.

Later, as I started practicing law, Dad's words proved to be prophetic, and I relied on them when preparing for trial, interviewing witnesses, and taking depositions. Like much of what he told me as a young boy that I discounted or ignored, he was right. People see what they want to see and have selective hearing, even when they are not trying to do so. It is human nature. And forget about hearsay—it usually has many layers of unreliable recollections, filtered through more selective hearing. So, when I train young litigators, those words are part of my mentoring speeches. "Like my father used to say . . ."

^ ^ ^ ^ ^

Between November 1943 and May 1944, the Nazis, using prisoners they captured from Cansano and the nearby towns of Campo di Giove and Pacentro, built trenches and buried explosive mines around the towns and in the mountains along trails and roads. They even placed explosives on railroads. The Cansanesi refugees living in the mountains often tripped mines, causing explosions that killed or maimed them. They could also hear the war being waged in the towns to the south of Cansano and in Sulmona to the north, but Cansano was relatively unscathed. My parents, staying closer to Sulmona, heard and saw more of the battles. Occasionally, Allied forces on a reconnaissance dropped aerial bombs on the outskirts of Cansano, destroying a few farmhouses. But the center of the town was largely saved.

Throughout Italy, the Allies engaged in aggressive bombardments, starting in the late summer of 1943 and escalating into 1944. This included the Battle of Monte Cassino just south of Cansano, which would become a central battle in the war. The Allies bombarded many parts of the country, focusing targets on industry, communications, and utilities. The country was destroyed and many civilians were killed. The country's infrastructure was obliterated, setting the tone for post-war struggles and massive emigration.

By April and May 1944, the war was getting closer to Cansano and Allied reconnaissance bombings became more frequent. At the same time, more of the Cansanese women and children—extremely malnourished and dirty—started moving back into the village to hide in the abandoned homes in *La Partayova*. The Nazis largely stayed away from this part of town, which had no electricity and was impossible to travel by military vehicles because of the steep and narrow streets. In the early days of the occupation, the Nazis did not tolerate anyone returning to the village. Those who tried early in the occupation were killed or sent to prisoner of war camps in Padua in the north or Castel Frentano, Atessa, Torricella Peligna, Alfedena, and Castel di Sangro to the south of Cansano.

In other parts of Italy, the Nazis were more tolerant and allowed the locals to return to their homes at night. But not the Nazis who occupied this part of Abruzzo. By April 1944, with the Allies approaching, the Nazi occupants of Cansano became less concerned about the locals' presence in town, focusing instead on the fast-approaching battles. At night, a few brave men snuck back into town as well to be with their wives and children. My mom's family was one of those that moved back early. They found their homes in shambles and their possessions all gone.

"Back at home, nothing was there," my mom recalled. "They took everything. My dad had to cut the trunk of the trees just to make chairs. We had to start over."

While returning home provided some comfort for the mountain evacuees, other dangers existed. The Cansano citizens were near the epicenter of World War II, and they had no idea that a major battle was brewing just to the south of their tiny village.

Another memory from my mom, one I heard many times and that she shared with Dante in 2018:

> When they [the Americans and British] was doing the bombardment, I was a little girl and used to go with my Uncle Tony to find food. The airplanes used to throw candy, some chocolates, and toys and drop them out the plane. My uncle would say, 'Don't touch that! It could be a bomb.' And many were bombs. You pick it up and boom—deformed face or killed or whatever. A little boy, about my age, maybe a little older, was killed in April or May 1944 by my house on *Via Roma* when he went to pick up a toy and it exploded. Why they have to do that?

As the Battle of Monte Cassino continued, the Nazis grew more desperate, blowing up bridges and rail lines and exploding mines on roads to make travel difficult for the Allied troops. Already isolated villages like Cansano became completely inaccessible.

The bombings increased, and the Allies used even more dangerous and questionable strategies to push the Nazis north. Another story from my mom:

> It was spring and we had nothing. My mom, who always used to take care of the small piece of land we had in the country to cultivate the wheat, corn, and potatoes, wanted to plant some things. But the Americans come in with the chemicals, throw it on the farm and infect the ground where we used to grow beautiful garden. The plants wouldn't grow any fruits or vegetables.

On May 17, 1944, the final battle for Monte Cassino occurred, and the Polish and British forces secured control of the ancient Benedictine sanctuary of Monte Cassino, which overlooked the valley entrance. Between January and May 1944, approximately 55,000 Allied and 20,000 Nazi troops lost their lives in the Battle of Monte Cassino. The town and many surrounding villages were completely destroyed. To add to the bloodshed, another 50,000 Allied troops lost their lives in the Battle of Anzio on the coastline.

The Nazis began retreating from all of the mountain villages. On May 18, 1944, Cansano was liberated. The Cansanesi who had returned to town, including my parents' families, were awakened by a large explosion. The Nazis simultaneously detonated numerous bombs around the village, destroying the electric station that provided electricity to parts of the town, several bridges, and the road to Sulmona. Water pipes, which had been installed in the '30s, were also severely damaged.

"We heard the explosion," my father told me. "I am not sure where it came from."

"It was like an earthquake," my mom described it. "Everything shook. We didn't know what happened."

But the Nazis had left, and my ancestral village was finally free.

As word spread through the valley and mountains, families, including my dad's family, returned to Cansano. They feared the worst, not knowing what the last six months and final explosion had done to their village. Unlike other villages, however, the town had been spared from destruction. But their homes were ransacked and a mess, and their food supplies and belongings were gone.

"The Nazi soldiers took everything away," my dad said. "The families who became their comrades and helped them—and there were a few—they did OK. You cannot blame them. They were trying to help their families. But my family didn't want to associate with them. My family wanted nothing to do with it, so we had deep poverty that we could not escape."

The spirits and souls of many Cansanesi were defeated and empty.

^ ^ ^ ^ ^

On that second morning of our June 2013 trip to Cansano, Dad reshares many of the stories of World War II as we walk up a winding road toward the train station above town. The air is crisp and we are seemingly the only people moving around town. We stop at a curve in the road. The view is breathtaking, revealing the entire town, and we can see the village of Pacentro and its one-thousand-year-old castle in the distance. The city of Sulmona is behind it. Native flowers of every color paint the landscape, and smoke circles out of some chimneys.

"When I was thirteen, fourteen, fifteen, me and my friends would hike this area and over the mountains behind the train station. We would hunt for mushrooms," Dad recalls. "Those were, simple, good times." Dad's descriptions of his childhood waver between the beauty of innocence and simplicity on the one hand and the cruelty of poverty and suffering on the other.

We get lost in conversation about the war, his childhood, and then their return to Cansano in May of 1944. On my left in the distance is the bridge I had seen the day before, and I wonder if it was damaged the morning of May 18, 1944.

"Juwaa, I don't know how to say it," my dad says of his return to the town on that May day.

"We were happy to be free, and the Nazis were gone. But it was misery and another misery was about to begin. But the poor people of that town worked together, shared, helped each other rebuild their lives from nothing. Nothing," he said again.

He went on. "Then we all emigrate to America, Canada, Australia and help each other more and build amazing lives from nothing. Can you imagine where we came from and where we are today?"

The winding road from Sulmona to Cansano, with Cansano perched on the invisible hill. PHOTO BY NICOLETTA RONDINELLA

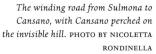

Late afternoon mist on the edge of Cansano, with the Maiella mountains on the right. PHOTO BY DANTE RUSCITTI

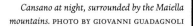

Cansano at night, surrounded by the Maiella mountains. PHOTO BY GIOVANNI GUADAGNOLI

Circa February 1958: The day my father emigrated to the US. Left to right: Zio Pietro, my father, Zio Armando, Zio Luciano, and Zia Anna in front.

The village sending my dad off to the US. Left to right, starting with the man in the white suit: Zio Pietro, my dad, Great-zio Rinaldo, Zio Luciano, Zio Armando, and Grandpa Rocco.

Circa 1954: My mom's family in Cansano. Left to right: my mom, Zia Liberta, Grandma Nunziata, Zia Angela (baby), Zio Luciano, Grandpa Panfilo, and Zia Emily.

March 28, 1957. Maria DiGiallonardo's and Emiliano Ruscitti's wedding day.

My parents in Frederick in the early 1960s.

Mom and Dad in Amalfi in 2013 (Above) and in Frederick in 2015 (Below).

Hunting rabbits in the late 1970s. Left to right: Zio Pietro, my dad, and me.

Sunrise Market in Berthoud in 1982. Left to Right: my sister Linda, my sister Rina, my sister Lora, my mom, my dad, and me.

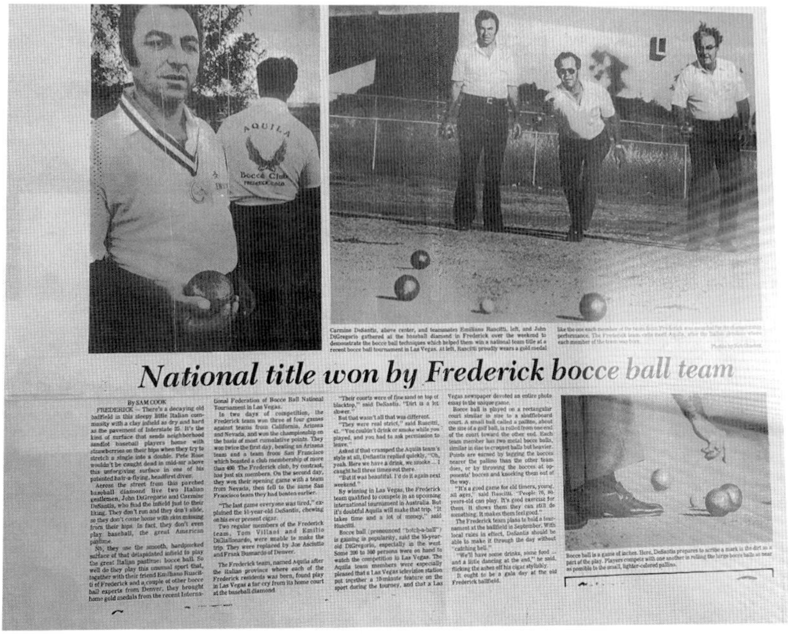

Carmine DeSantis, above center, and teammates Emiliano Ruscitti, left, and John DiGregorio gathered at the baseball diamond in Frederick over the weekend to demonstrate the bocce ball techniques which helped them win a national team title at a recent bocce ball tournament in Las Vegas. At left, Ruscitti proudly wears a gold medal like the one each member of the [illegible] performance. The Frederick team [illegible] Aquila, after the Italian [illegible] each member of the team was born.

National title won by Frederick bocce ball team

By SAM COOK

FREDERICK — There's a decaying old ballfield in this sleepy little Italian community with a clay infield as dry and hard as the pavement of Interstate 25. It's the kind of surface that sends neighborhood sandlot baseball players home with strawberries on their hips when they try to stretch a single into a double. Pete Rose wouldn't be caught dead in mid-air above this unforgiving surface in one of his patented hair-a-flying, headfirst dives.

Across the street from this parched baseball diamond live two Italian gentlemen, John DiGregorio and Carmine DeSantis, who find the infield just to their liking. They don't run and they don't slide, so they don't come home with skin missing from their hips. In fact, they don't even play baseball, the great American pastime.

No, they use the smooth, hardpacked surface of that delapidated infield to play the great Italian pastime: bocce ball. So well do they play this unusual sport that, together with their friend Emiliano Ruscitti of Frederick and a couple of other bocce ball experts from Denver, they brought home gold medals from the recent International Federation of Bocce Ball National Tournament in Las Vegas.

In two days of competition, the Frederick team won three of four games against teams from California, Arizona and Nevada, and won the championship on the basis of most cumulative points. They won twice the first day, beating an Arizona team and a team from San Francisco which boasted a club membership of more than 400. The Frederick club, by contrast, has just six members. On the second day, they won their opening game with a team from Nevada, then fell to the same San Francisco team they had beaten earlier.

"The last game everyone was tired," explained the 51-year-old DeSantis, chewing on his ever present cigar.

Two regular members of the Frederick team, Tom Villani and Emilio DiGiallonardo, were unable to make the trip. They were replaced by Joe Ascutto and Frank Busnardo of Denver.

The Frederick team, named Aquila after the Italian province where each of the Frederick residents was born, found play in Las Vegas a far cry from its home court at the baseball diamond.

"Their courts were of fine sand on top of blacktop," said DeSantis. "Dirt is a lot slower."

But that wasn't all that was different.

"They were real strict," said Ruscitti, 42. "You couldn't drink or smoke while you played, and you had to ask permission to leave."

Asked if that cramped the Aquila team's style at all, DeSantis replied quickly, "Oh, yeah. Here we have a drink, we smoke ... I caught hell three times out there.

"But it was beautiful. I'd do it again next weekend."

By winning in Las Vegas, the Frederick team qualified to compete in an upcoming international tournament in Australia. But it's doubtful Aquila will make that trip. "It takes time and a lot of money," said Ruscitti.

Bocce ball (pronounced "botch-a-ball") is gaining in popularity, said the 55-year-old DiGregorio, especially in the west. Some 200 to 300 persons were on hand to watch the competition in Las Vegas. The Aquila team members were especially pleased that a Las Vegas television station put together a 10-minute feature on the sport during the tourney, and that a Las Vegas newspaper devoted an entire photo essay to the unique game.

Bocce ball is played on a rectangular court similar in size to a shuffleboard court. A small ball called a pallino, about the size of a golf ball, is rolled from one end of the court toward the other end. Each team member has two metal bocce balls, similar in size to croquet balls but heavier. Points are earned by lagging the bocces nearer the pallino than the other team does, or by throwing the bocces at opponents' bocces and knocking them out of the way.

"It's a good game for old timers, young, all ages," said Ruscitti. "People 70, 80-years-old can play. It's good exercise for them. It shows them they can still do something. It makes them feel good."

The Frederick team plans to hold a tournament at the ballfield in September. With local rules in effect, DeSantis should be able to make it through the day without "catching hell."

"We'll have some drinks, some food ... and a little dancing at the end," he said, flicking the ashes off his cigar stylishly.

It ought to be a gala day at the old Frederick ballfield.

Bocce ball is a game of inches. Here, DeSantis prepares to scribe a mark in the dirt as a part of the play. Players compete with one another in rolling the large bocce balls as near as possible to the small, lighter-colored pallino.

US National Bocce Champions in 1979.

Having a glass of wine with my dad in Frederick (Above left). PHOTO BY DANTE RUSCITTI.
The fountain across the street from my mom's childhood home (Above right).

My father standing in front of his childhood home in 2013.

My dad looking at the window where his cousin jumped to his death to avoid capture by the Nazis in November 1943.

The piazza of Cansano, with the monument of the fallen soldiers in front, the municipal building in the background, and the Maiella mountains on the right.

The steep cobblestone stairwell in La Partayova.

The amber lights of Cansano. Via Casale on the way from the piazza to Zio Pietro's home.

CHAPTER TWENTY-ONE

Food and Wine

The San Giovanni religious procession starts at the *Chiesa di San Rocco* in the piazza and comes up *Via dell'Emigrante,* the Street of Immigrants, before turning left on *Via Roma* in front of my mom's childhood house, my uncle's house, and my cousin's bed-and-breakfast. Several men carry a statue of Saint Giovanni, which sits on a flat pedestal adorned with gold-and-silver ornaments. In front of the statue is a group of altar boys and girls dressed in white robes and carrying Bibles and small candles, followed by a marching band playing religious music, and then the priest of the *Chiesa di San Rocco*. As the procession moves through town and past homes, residents and visitors of all ages stand on the streets and people join to form a large parade. Some of the townspeople are dressed up in their Sunday church clothes. No one seems to be working today, and most of the town and its guests, including us, join the parade. Aside from the band and the sound of crunching rocks on the cobblestones, it is strangely quiet, people honoring the moment. We gently walk down *Via Casale,* which narrows through several homes and then turns left. The group moves into the piazza, and some daytime fireworks go off in the distance. It is a lovely June morning, and the smoke from the fireworks lingers in the blue sky. People mingle and the two *vinerie* in town fill up, and the wine and beer flow. It is about eleven o'clock in the morning and no one is in a hurry. Except me—we have my schedule to stick to. I want to visit Pescocostanzo.

It is time for a day trip, and I want to get to Pescocostanzo before the *riposo* starts. After Pescocostanzo, we would drive back to Sulmona for a late lunch and then a tour of a winery in Popoli arranged by a master sommelier friend back home. My uncle is unable to join us—more deliveries to make to restaurants for San Giovanni celebrations that evening.

The drive out of Cansano to Pescocostanzo delivers a beauty I have not seen before. The road out of town steeply climbs the Maiella mountains, offering another spectacular view of Cansano below. The road flattens and meanders through a forest of tall, leafy trees that are different from those on the drive from Sulmona to Cansano. Suddenly, the trees on each side connect, creating a thick green canopy over the road. Rays of sunlight slip through the leaves, creating an almost magical scene.

"Wow, look how beautiful, Dad," Izabella says.

"I have never seen anything like it," I respond.

We emerge from the tree awning through a lush forest and drive past numerous roadside farmhouses. My dad and cousin are deep in a conversation about local politics, and the road enters a large meadow that looks like it's straight out of a classic Italian painting. The bucolic countryside and framed rolling hills surround the road. The Maiella mountains rise high above the rolling hills on both sides of the road. The road is lined with well-manicured fields and crops. A rainbow of colorful flowers and crops dot the "*campagna*," or countryside.

Even though I had not yet been to Tuscany, I knowingly say in Italian, "This looks like Tuscany."

"Tuscany is beautiful," Rocco responds in Italian. "But Abruzzo is the jewel of Italy. Undiscovered by tourists."

And he was right. When talking about Italy, people talk about Rome, Milan, Tuscany, Florence, Cinque Terre, Venice, Piedmont, Naples, the Amalfi, and Sicily. No one talks about Abruzzo. In the years to come, we visited and loved most of these places, each offering something different. Rome is a city of "wows," with its rich history and magnificent religious and cultural monuments. Every street you turn on offers an indescribable view of history, art, architecture, and culture. The cuisine is simpler in Rome than in Tuscany, which we visited in 2017 with Dante, Donato, and Izabella. Tuscany is an expansive stretch of land in north-central Italy known for its soft, rolling hills and Cyprus tree-framed vineyards and roads, the focal points of which are cities like art- and culture-rich Florence and Siena. The landscape is alive with vineyards, olive groves, and sunflowers. Tuscany's famous Sangiovese grapes grown near and around the medieval town of Montalcino have made Chianti and Brunello some of the most famous wines in the world.

To the northwest sits Cinque Terre, a quintet of coastal towns that sit on the steep mountains overlooking the Italian Riviera. It is a lot like Amalfi, which we visited in 2013 and is south of Rome and east of Naples; both are bursting with breathtaking views of the sea. Amalfi is known for its lemons that are the size of an orange and cuisine that is centered on fresh fish. And sophisticated Piedmont is further north of Cinque Terre, surrounded by the Alps. It is the home to truffles and the "king of grapes," the Nebbiolo grape, which is used to make our favorite wines, Barolo and Barbaresco. Aggie and I visited this region in October of 2019 in time for the wine harvest and truffle festival. The views, food, and wine were, in a word, spectacular. It is like Tuscany, but not. The rolling hills and vineyards are more pronounced—a quilt of vineyards, hazelnut groves, and colorful flowers—with the Alps in the distance that soar ethereally into the clouds. And the food and wine are, simply put, heavenly. And then there is Venice, which we also visited in 2019. We expected a city overflowing with tourists but instead found a romantic maze of water streets bordered by small sidewalks and buildings built on piers that leave you wondering in amazement at how they were built (and why). Nestled between the water streets were shops and restaurants, including a hidden gem that had the best pasta dish we had ever had—a simple and light marinara sauce with bay shrimp (so good that we had the dish for lunch and dinner on the same day).

But Abruzzo is different. The pace is slower. Enchanting. The people are not less intelligent or sophisticated but simpler and more inviting. The food is peasant, focused on basic and local ingredients. The hilltop towns are unassuming, quiet, and quaint. The churches are smaller but equally historic and magnificent, with ornamental canopies and domes, paintings, sculptures, marble, woodwork, and other artistry that matches the more famous churches in Rome and Florence. Its wines, Montepulciano d'Abruzzo and Trebbiano d'Abruzzo, are less pretentious than their cousins to the north but full of flavor and character. Known as "the greenest region in Europe," half of Abruzzo's territory is preserved as national parks and protected nature reserves. The landscape is more diverse and greener, with the rugged Apennine Mountains, vineyards from Sulmona up to L'Aquila and down to the coastal town of Pescara, and miles of beaches along the Adriatic Sea.

^ ^ ^ ^ ^

The winding road hugs the base of the mountain as we approach Pescocostanzo. Like Cansano, Pescocostanzo is over one thousand years old, rich with history and local tradition. Unlike Cansano, Pescocostanzo is prospering, which I notice as soon as we walk into town. The buildings look just like the buildings in Cansano, with the same Renaissance-style architecture and made from the same local materials of limestone and timber. But they have been well-maintained and none are falling apart. The main street entering into the center of town is lined with rows of homes and charming little *bottegas*, or shops—pastry shops, bakeries, and art stores. Mixed in are a few artisanal shops where handmade iron goods, lace, and jewelry are made and sold. Several small hotels, restaurants, cafés, and wine shops dot the main street, named *Via Roma* (every town in Italy seems to have a *Via Roma*).

"I love this town," Donato says as we walk up the street and visit several of the *botteghe*.

We returned here many times over the years and enjoyed some of the simplest, yet finest, meals I have ever had at a small restaurant named *Il*

Gallo di Pietra inside the *Hotel Le Torri*. We celebrated Izabella's fifteenth birthday there in 2014 with my parents, and, in 2017, I had one of my top five meals ever at *Il Gallo*—a simple polenta with lamb sausage, mushrooms, shallots, and olive oil, with a nice Italian chardonnay.

Perhaps it was his lack of food and his life in poverty as a child, but my father had a romance with food that I didn't appreciate until these trips to Italy. During our hunting and fishing trips when I was a young boy, lunch was almost the most important part of the experience. My dad and uncles brought a larger cooler with enough food to last a week—dried sausage, prosciutto, mortadella, cheeses, pasta dishes, marinated peppers, pickled vegetables, crusty bread, marinated olives, and chicken, goat, or lamb cacciatore with more potatoes and red and green peppers. And wine. All homemade. And they brought an abundance of seasonal fresh fruit—cantaloupe, watermelon, peaches, plums, or apricots. If it was watermelon season and we were near a river, the watermelon chilled in the river before it was served. If American friends joined us, they quickly abandoned their bologna-and-cheese sandwiches and potato chips and joined the Ruscitti feast.

"Throw away that junk," my dad told his friends of their packed American lunch. "This is the real food."

With the pocketknife he always carried, Dad would cut some homemade bread and a chunk of provolone cheese. He'd layer the cheese on the bread with some prosciutto, mortadella, and marinated peppers. He would hand it to me with a small amount of wine in a Styrofoam cup with some 7 Up soda. It was the best sandwich I ever had.

Our lunches on these trips lasted an hour or two. I watched my dad carefully peel a peach, slice it, and put a few slices into his wine. This was something he and his brother Armando always did. I have never seen anyone do it since. He then ate other slices of his peach off his knife, with bites of my mom's bread, dried sausages, and cheese in between. "This is food," he would say. Later in life he did the same thing when we took my boys fishing, and he relished being able to cook for his grandchildren and his friends.

"Dad, what are you doing?" I would call and ask on my way home from the office.

Against the background of chatter and laughter he would say, "Oh, the neighbors came over. We are having some food. I grilled some steaks, cut some prosciutto and sausage, and your mom made some sauce and pasta. And some wine. Just something small and fast."

Their kitchen table was a social event.

^ ^ ^ ^ ^

Except for Rome, where we found most of the food to be ordinary, the food in Italy is rich and full of flavor, with the best meals coming from hidden gems that are off the beaten path. In 2019, Aggie and I ate at *Ristorante Dulcis Vitis*, a Michelin restaurant in Alba in central Piedmont. When we arrived at our bed-and-breakfast on our first day in Alba in 2019 for the beginning of the International Alba White Truffle Fair, we were greeted by a disheveled man named Pietro Giovannini, who introduced himself as the owner of the property. Seemingly disinterested in us, he tried to check us in as quickly as possible. I started talking Italian to him, telling him my parents were from Abruzzo. Something I had learned during our many trips over the years was that the mention of my family's local roots would ingratiate me to locals. After that mention, everything changed.

"What are your plans?" he asked in Italian. And before I could answer, he said, "I will take care of you."

Like a mad scientist, he sent several texts and made a few calls. "You are all set. Today you will tour a vineyard owned by my good friend Alberto in La Morra, which is a small area in Piedmont. I have a driver for you, and she will take you to a wine tasting also. And tomorrow she will take you on a tour of a vineyard owned by my friend Davide near Barbaresco. And you will have dinner tomorrow night with my friend Bruno. You will love him. And the next day after, we will see."

The next night, we arrived at *Ristorante Dulcis Vitis* after a day of driving through Piedmont and drinking wine. It was my birthday. A perfect day. The restaurant was small, and I noticed the red brick ceiling. After I selected a bottle of Barolo—one of the best I ever drank—the sommelier carefully "seasoned" our wine glasses, pouring a small amount of wine from another bottle of Barolo and then turning the glass at an angle and slowly rotating the glass to allow the wine to crawl up the glass. We were entranced. Reading my mind, he said in Italian, "This will remove any impurities left over from washing the glass. So, you taste nothing but the wine."

Chef and owner Bruno Cingolani then came to our table. A rotund man with a bald head, he exuberantly and cheerily greeted us in Italian, "You are friends with Pietro? I will take care of you." He asked us what we liked to eat, and then made a delectable multicourse off-menu dinner starting with a salad of thinly sliced white mushrooms with olive oil, salt, black pepper, and shaved fresh truffles. How could something so simple be so indescribably good?

We had a similar experience in Pacentro in 2017 with the children. After a tour of the ancient town nestled on the side of the mountain, we asked someone on the street for a place to eat and they pointed lazily toward a small street off the piazza. After circling around the area, we walked into *Taverna de li Caldora*, a restaurant with no sign or awning. A small sign on the window saying that it had a Michelin star was the only indication it was a restaurant. A man walked up and I chatted him up in Italian, which by 2017 I knew was the way to be treated as a local. I told him we were visiting my family in Cansano just a few miles away. He said he went to school with my cousin Rocco. He said he was the owner and, like Bruno did in Alba, he walked us through the fresh ingredients he had in the kitchen that day—lamb from my uncle's ranch, some fresh fish from nearby Pescara, and some vegetables and herbs from the garden he pointed to on the side of the mountain. He asked us all what we liked to eat. No menu. They made seven separate entrées, off menu, from scratch.

In Siena in 2017, we were starved after a morning of touring the city that rivaled Rome and Florence for power and prestige centuries ago.

We walked off Piazza del Campo and saw a small restaurant on the right named *La Taverna di San Giuseppe.* As we read the menu on the window, a bird pooped on Aggie—a great sign in Italy, meaning you will be blessed with health and prosperity.

"It is a sign, let's eat here," I exclaimed. And wow.

Owned by father-and-son chefs Marco and Matteo, this was not just another Michelin restaurant—it was a walk back in time. The interior had an almost rounded vaulted ceiling with terra-cotta-colored bricks, which sat on top of whitewashed walls made with local limestone that was chipping away in parts. A stone staircase at the back of the restaurant takes you to a cavernous, underground room built two thousand years ago, now used as a wine cellar and for private wine-and-cheese tastings. I was immediately brought back to grandfather Panfilo's wine cellar on Second Street in Frederick, Colorado. The same wet stone, damp and wet earth, old wood, cork, and musk smell overcame me. As stunning as the room was, the food was even better. My risotto with a lamb ragù still makes my mouth water as I write this.

We had similar stories all over Italy—Michelin restaurants hidden in the smallest of towns and off untraveled streets.

"Treat people right and they will always take care of you," my father told me as a child. And he did and they did. His home was open to everyone, and he loved sharing what he had.

I followed my father's advice, and the owners of the restaurants all over Italy quickly became my best friends, as were restaurant owners in Boulder, Denver, and New York. "Please come back," they would say in Italian. "You are welcome here any time. You are family."

"You are a *chiacchierone* just like your dad," Aggie said during our 2019 trip.

Zio Pietro had my father's charm as well. In 2019, Aggie, Zio Pietro, and I went to Pescocostanzo hoping to have the mushroom polenta I had had in 2017 at *Il Gallo di Pietra*.

"Zio, it is best polenta you will ever have," I told him in Italian.

Chuckling, he indulged me. "*Va bene*," he said. "Sounds good."

To my disappointment, they were closed, so we walked into a small but packed restaurant named *Ristorante da Paolino*. The room was filled with businessmen and women on their lunch breaks from nearby towns.

"They don't buy lamb or cheese from me, but that is OK," my uncle said in Italian.

We were greeted by the owner, a distinguished-looking older woman in her mid-sixties. My zio, who was always stylishly dressed, had grown into a very handsome octogenarian and looked twenty years younger than he was. He was calm, confident, and charming without trying. This day, he wore dark brown tweed-like trousers, a button-up wool dress shirt, and a dark vest. You would never know he was a rancher.

"My name is Pietro Ruscitti from Cansano," my uncle said in Italian, flashing a smile. "I have the best lamb and pecorino cheese in Abruzzo. I will bring you some to try."

The owner seated us at their best table, obviously enamored with my uncle. We enjoyed another mouthwatering and delicious meal—some simple risotto and pasta dishes with their house red wine in a carafe.

CHAPTER TWENTY-TWO

The Phone Call

It is April 12, 2017. I am at the office reviewing a construction contract. My cell phone rings from a number I don't recognize. I normally would not answer a call from a number I don't recognize, but this time I have a feeling I should.

"Giovanni, this is Doctor Smith, your dad's doctor. How are you?"

"Good," I say, but, knowing my dad had his doctor appointment today, I am wondering why he's calling me.

"Well, your dad got some tests last week because of his weight loss and fatigue, and we got the results back. I am here with him and your mom, and he wants me to explain them to you."

Anxiety overcomes me. This can't be good if the doctor is calling to explain this to me.

"Our tests show he has some blockage in his bile ducts. It may just be some stones, but we need to do some additional tests to rule out some other things."

What the heck is a bile duct? I google bile duct and bile duct diseases as he continues to talk.

"The leading doctors for bile duct issues are at UC Health in Denver. I have made an appointment for him on the twentieth at six o'clock in the morning. You will need to take him, as they need to do some tests and he will not be able to drive home."

The first few websites are not encouraging. "OK. Is this serious?"

"Well, we don't know. That is why we are doing the tests. They will do an endoscopic ultrasound and that will tell us if it is stones or something to worry about. But, other than the weight loss and loss of energy, he is in excellent shape for an eighty-one-year-old."

Endoscopic? What is that? I quickly google endoscopic ultrasound. A test used to, among other things, diagnose certain types of cancer. Fuck.

I had never thought of my dad as weak or about him dying. He was very strong and full of energy. He was the strongest man I knew. I knew, of course, he wouldn't live forever, but death wasn't something I thought about. First Rina and now this? At the same time? I think about my mom. I was able to get my sister into MD Anderson to see the leading inflammatory breast cancer doctor in the country, but during the process we learned that the diagnosis was likely a death sentence. Most likely not *if* but *when*. My mom was devastated, and I was worried this news about my dad would put her over the top.

"Anything else I should know, doctor?"

"Let's talk when we get the results."

"Thanks, Doctor Smith."

CHAPTER TWENTY-THREE

Pescocostanzo

We find ourselves in Pescocostanzo on San Giovanni Day in 2013. All of the small towns have similar street names, and Pescocostanzo is no different. The town's version of *Via Roma* is a narrow one-way street, with a white-and-black cobblestone arrow design directing you to the main piazza and fountain. The piazza is surrounded by the town municipal building and more shops and restaurants. The town has a distinct artistic feel. After some photographs, we walk down another street toward a nondescript-looking building.

"*Buongiorno*," we say and hear back many times, and a hushed buzz of conversation softly fills the street like background music in a quiet restaurant. A few locals meander about, some going in and out of shops, some standing and deep in conversations, and others making deliveries of local products to the shops. I am captivated by their friendliness, and no one is in a hurry like back home. As we reach some steps leading up to the old building at the end of the street, I turn and watch the gentle orchestrated wave of the locals' quiet and peaceful existence.

We climb the stairs and enter *Basilica di Santa Maria del Colle*, a church originally built in the eleventh century and rebuilt in the 1400s after it was destroyed by an earthquake. A few old women dressed in all black, including black lace scarves draped over their heads, are kneeling and praying at altars close to the crucifix. This is an Italian thing from generations past—my grandmother Filomena wore black every day of her life after my grandfather Rocco died in 1965. She lived until 1998 and would occasionally mix things up by wearing a dark navy blue sweater instead of black.

While I grew up Catholic, taking confirmation and going to church with my grandmother Filomena, I am no longer a practicing Catholic, choosing instead to follow a spiritual path that finds truth and common ground in most of the world religions.

During this trip and the trips to come, I learned that churches are not just a place of worship in Italy. They are pieces of art. *Basilica di Santa Maria del Colle* was stunning. Several arched terra-cotta walls divide the church into multiple areas of worship with separate altarpieces, each decorated with vibrant inlaid marble. The main ceiling is carved, golden wood with intricate designs. The crucifix is a true work of art, with exquisitely carved wood and vibrant gold touches.

As we walk out of the church and grab an espresso at a bar next to the church, I ask Rocco, *"Cugino, questa città è diversa da Cansano, è piu prospera. Perchè?"* (Cousin, this town is different from Cansano, very prosperous. Why?)

"The war hit Cansano harder for some reason and over one thousand people emigrated from the town in the late '40s, '50s, and '60s," he responds in Italian. "And many towns like Pescocostanzo acted early to preserve their towns and build tourism. That did not happen in Cansano."

"E oro sta morendo," he continues. "And now it is dying."

Fast-forward to 2021. My family's past collides with the present and, perhaps, my future. There is a movement in Cansano led by the new mayor and town council to renovate *La Partayova* and other abandoned parts of town. The plan includes giving notice to the families that own the old properties and giving them a deadline to renovate the homes. If not, the properties will be condemned and sold to investors to renovate the area. The plan is complicated, as Italian laws dictate that the old properties are owned by all of the living heirs of the titled property owners, meaning that distant relatives who have never met or even know of each other's existence each own fractional shares of the dilapidated, abandoned properties. Finding all of them, much less getting consensus from a potentially large, disparate group across the world, seems like a failed plan and one that will undoubtedly lead to the town condemning the properties.

For example, the property records show that my great-grandfather Cassiodoro Ruscitti owned several properties in *La Partayova*. So, all of his heirs have a fractional interest in the properties. But he had six sons, including my grandfather Rocco. One stayed in Italy, four moved to Australia, and my grandfather moved to the United States. They are all deceased. So, ownership resides in their heirs. This is where it starts getting tricky. Many of their heirs are deceased, so you have to go to their heirs. Unfortunately, some of those people have also passed, so their shares go to their heirs. And so on. So, this means potentially hundreds of people, most of whom I don't know and have no way of reaching, own fractional shares of a property. Getting consensus from this group will be impossible.

As I read about the plan in public forums, heated exchanges ensue, with one group blaming all of the emigrants (like my family) for abandoning the town and causing not only the condition of the old part of town but also the town's overall economic collapse. Another group, mostly the descendants of the emigrants, blame town leadership over the years for poor planning and the failure to attract business and tourism to the town as the other communities in the region have successfully done.

I reach out to the mayor and a councilman, whom I later learned was a distant relative, and obtain information about the plan, both for and against. I am torn. The idea, in concept, is a good one. The area needs renovation and the town needs something to stimulate the local economy and tourism. I think back to what Rocco told me in 2013 and wonder why emigration hit Cansano harder than the other towns. The town needs a stimulus; otherwise, it will soon die as each member of the World War II generation passes away. There are only a few left alive.

On the other hand, I feel a deep connection to the area and my family roots and wonder what will be done. I am worried that a part of me that

I just discovered is about to be taken away. It's more than just a place, more than old buildings falling to the ground. It feels sacred. It tells my story. It is my story. It's part of who I am.

"I like the plan, but it's important to maintain the architecture and history of the area," I tell the mayor. "It's also important to make sure that the families of the emigrants, who were only trying to find a better life for themselves and their future heirs, have a voice in the process and the ability to participate somehow."

He agrees. But I still feel like something is about to be taken away from me. I wonder if this is a calling for me and if I should get more involved. I don't have any time. At all.

I offer to help. The mayor accepts.

TWENTY-FOUR

The Serenade

We cap off San Giovanni Day with a late-afternoon wine tasting event in Popoli and follow it up with more family time and another multicourse meal in Cansano. After the meal, we walk down to the piazza to catch the end of the San Giovanni Day celebration. Even though less than three hundred people live here, the little town is vibrant and full of life at night, and it is a late night. A live band plays Italian gypsy favorites. The town celebrates three straight days of saints. Tomorrow is San Antonio's Day, and the next day is San Nicola's Day. Visitors from the United States and Canada, as well as locals from Sulmona and other towns, fill the two *vinerie* and the main restaurant in town. I walk into the restaurant, *Ara Del Colle*, and buy a bottle of local Montepulciano di Abruzzo wine to take out to the piazza. "Can you imagine being able to do that back home?" I later return for a second bottle of wine as a small group of us enjoys the festivities. Izabella and Donato make friends with the youth their age and are out exploring the town. Music and conversation fill the crisp air, and a fresh mountain fragrance that blends with the scent of burning timber from fireplaces overcomes me. As we sit in the piazza, I feel content and relaxed.

It was a late night, and I wake up on our third day a little later than I did the last two days. I miss our morning walk, but I feel renewed. My jet lag seems to be settling down, and I am beginning to see a side of my father I have never seen. He is at home and feeling comfortable. I also truly hear him for the first time. I feel a sense of belonging that I did not expect to be feeling—and that I have never felt anywhere else before.

Everyone is up, and after the traditional Italian breakfast of coffee and cookies, we all walk up *Via Roma* from the kitchen area of the bed-and-breakfast. We see an old woman who appears to be in her nineties dressed in black sitting outside my mom's childhood home. My dad recognizes the woman. She is a Ruscitti (she married one of his cousins, long since deceased) and my dad tells the woman that this was my mom's childhood home and that my mom had not been in the home since 1954. The old woman immediately invites us all in and offers us food, which we politely decline. The home has been remodeled, but my mom recognizes many aspects of the home, including the fireplace, terra-cotta limestone walls, and stairwell up to the second floor. She tells us about each room. We then walk out to a massive deck that overlooks the cavernous valley below.

"I used to serenade your mom from right there," my dad says, pointing to an area below the deck. They have been married almost sixty years.

In 2018, my mom told Dante and Donato the same story she has told many times before.

> In Cansano, there wasn't enough work after the war. My Uncle Tony, Grandpa Falco, and another uncle, they came over here to America in 1947. We stayed, and my dad worked any job to help the family. My mom used to take care of the house and the land, a piece of land we had in the country to cultivate the wheat, corn, and potatoes.

As I look over the valley from the deck, I remember the story and wonder where the land is. My mom's story continues:

> Then, in 1948, my grandpa Falco decided he wanted to come back to Italy. He made some money working in the coal mines, and he wrote a letter to my dad saying, 'I'm going to come back and stay in Italy.' And then he came back. He had a little money. I

> don't know how much he had. He had five sons. He spent a little money and gave some to my dad and his sons. My dad said, 'You know I always wanted to buy some cows.' So, he bought some cows that we would milk and sell for extra money. Not a lot of people had fresh milk in the late '40s and early '50s. And that is how I met your dad.

"I met your mom at a very early age—maybe ten or twelve years old," my dad says as we look out over the valley.

"He used to come and buy milk," Mom says.

"My mom was sick and the doctor recommended sheep milk or goat milk because it was lighter than the other milk. Maria's family had a cow—no, two cows," my dad tells Aggie. "So, we got to know each other. Maybe she liked me—I don't know—but I bought their milk."

"I was embarrassed. I was young and I thought, 'Who is this boy who keeps coming to buy milk?' But he was so handsome."

"When she saw me, she wanted no contact with me. She was all bashful. She would run away!" my dad laughs.

"I would see him everywhere. Buying milk, in the piazza—everywhere."

"Me and two friends, Concetto Morelli and Donato Serna, we all lived in *La Partayova*. Concetto's family lived in the little home above ours. They were very poor. We used to go around at nighttime, and I used to play the harmonica. We used to go serenade the girls we liked. Me to your mom and Concetto and Donato to their girlfriends. I played the harmonica, they sang. Augustino Villani would play with us also."

"The first time, he went to my mom's balcony, and not mine," my mom says. "The neighbor, an old man, said, 'Young man, that is not her balcony. That is her mom's balcony.'"

They laugh.

"Donato Serna married his girlfriend also. Her name was Eda and she was one of my best friends," my mom says. "Concetto liked Helen DiSalle, another one of my best friends. But her dad did not like Concetto's family. 'The family is too poor,' he would say. That is too bad; Concetto is such a nice man. But he married a nice woman from here."

"Concetto and Donato live in Canada. I still talk to them all the time," my dad says. "We sang whatever. We would go over to the balcony. At nighttime, the harmonica sounded beautiful, and you could hear the echo across the big valley," he says, pointing down the valley.

"'Go away,' I would yell at them. I was embarrassed."

"The echo would come back to us and just sounded beautiful. Anyway, at the end, we got married," Dad laughs, as if we didn't know.

"My dad and his dad were friends," Mom continues. "They would have a drink in the piazza together, and I would go with my dad. Rocco would say, 'You are a very beautiful young lady. My son likes you.' I was so young."

"That was a different time. That is the way it was," my dad says.

"I moved to the United States with my dad, my sister Liberta, and my brother Louie in 1954," my mom says. "My mom and sisters Angela and Emily stayed in Cansano. We didn't have enough money for everyone to come. They came in 1956."

"She came back to marry me in 1957 and then she came back to America. I moved to America in 1958 after I got a sponsor. We got married at a fairly young age. I was a week short of twenty-one, and she was almost eighteen."

CHAPTER TWENTY-FIVE

Love Letters

My parents were a gorgeous young couple. As a teen, my mom was tall, slender, and beautiful. Her skin was like porcelain, and her shoulder-length black hair, dark and deep brown eyes, high cheek bones, and smaller Roman nose evoked a young Sophia Loren. Izabella resembled her, especially when she got older. "She was so pretty," my dad told Dante and Donato in 2018. "But look at us now. We are old and no longer good looking," he laughs.

My dad was five foot ten with a lean, almost sinewy build. He had thick, dark wavy hair and green eyes with a hint of yellow, almost cat-like. With his strong jaw, he had that classic Italian male look. When he dressed up, which he liked to do often, he had a Hollywood air about him. He could have been a model.

As we stand on the balcony of my mom's childhood home in Cansano, a memory surfaces. In the '70s, my parents went dancing on many weekends. They both dressed up—my father in a suit, tie, and ever-present fedora, and my mom in a colorful dress. They went to the Shangri-La Dance Club in north Denver, a popular entertainment club for Italian Americans. I had completely forgotten about their dancing.

"I still have my wedding dress, Bella," my mom tells Izabella on the balcony that June morning. "You are built like me. Maybe you can wear my dress when you get married."

"Let's see if we can go into the church we got married in," she continues.

Over the years, Dad continued to serenade Mom, playing her favorite song, "Spanish Eyes," on the harmonica, especially when he'd had a glass or two of wine.

We all slowly walk down *Via Oriente* and through the twisting streets that lead up a steep walkway to *La Chiesa Madre di San Salvatore*. The church is on *Via Castello*, the highest point in the village near an old castle.

"The way we did it back then, your dad and his family and friends walked to my house," my mom says. "His mom brought my wedding veil and a basket of pizzelles for my mom. And then we walked to the church, the same path we just took."

She pauses. "Yup, that is the way we did it back then."

"Look at the castle," my dad says. "The great baronial families of Abruzzo had castles in all the towns they controlled. They lived in this castle over one thousand years ago. Marble everywhere, engraved wood. I went in there a few times when I was a boy. I don't think we can get in. It is probably dangerous."

Pointing up, "The tower that overlooks the whole valley. The *barone* (rich owner) would be on the lookout for the early *briganti* (bandits). They would ring the large bell in the tower if there was trouble."

The church is, like the rest of *La Partayova*, weathered. Built in the early 1300s, the church was nearly destroyed by a large earthquake in 1706. The locals, with the help of the Catholic Church, rebuilt the church in classic basilica style, with three naves, or sections, that run from the rear of the church to the crucifix. The wood door is bordered by an engraved marble that is blackened by the elements. The exterior of the church is made with rocks from the local quarries. The building looks aged and sad.

"Can we go in?" Izabella asks.

My dad tries to open the door. "I don't think so," my dad responds. "There was a big earthquake in 2009, and they say it is not safe. I will see if the mayor will let us in."

Later, I learned that, unlike some of the other churches in the region with painted ceilings, the arched ceiling of *La Chiesa Madre di San Salvatore* is a simple yet masterfully engraved limestone-and-marble work of art. The church was once home to a massive and intricately designed silver censer built in the fifteenth century. It drew the attention of artists and dignitaries for centuries. But, like the rest of the village, it disappeared during or after World War II.

The outside and inside of the church represent the rugged nature of the local Cansanesi—not flashy, but simple and strong. A sense of sadness, which became more familiar as I walked through *La Partayova* in my later trips and think about my ancestors' lives, overcomes me as I look at the church and castle. I wonder why the town—and I guess part of my heritage—was not maintained. What led the Cansanese, including my family, to completely abandon everything they had ever known for the unknown? I remember again the story my dad often told of his great-grandfather, who left Italy for the United States in the 1800s only to return to Cansano saying, "I left a civilized country and found the wild west that was uncivilized!"

My parents hold hands outside the church. I don't think I have ever seen them hold hands before. By 2013, they have grown into a more affectionate couple, having never before displayed any affection. While my dad was more gregarious, my mom was quiet and guarded, unwilling to share emotions.

"Why does Grandma never smile in pictures?" my children or my nieces often asked. Perhaps her hard exterior hid a rough childhood and the struggles of moving to and assimilating into America. And, candidly, their early years were not always easy. They were products of a different time, and I despised the Italian machismo culture I observed in my childhood and teens with my dad and his brothers. This shaped the man I would become and, more importantly, who I didn't want to be.

By 2013, my dad's edges were softened; when he sensed my mom being rigid, he playfully teased her until she smiled or softened.

"*Guagliò*, why do you have to be so mean?" he would ask if she was on edge. *Guaglione* means friend in Italian, and it was usually used by men when talking to other friends. Many Italian immigrants, including my dad and other Cansanese men in Frederick, pronounced it "wall-yo." But for some reason, he would call my mom "wall-yo" and he referred to her so much that way that my close friends in high school would all call each other wall-yo.

"It's because you driva me crazy," she would respond with a smile. "Leave me alone."

Or they engaged in a back-and-forth, almost like the George Burns and Gracie Allen comedy routine from the '60s.

"Have you had too much wine to drink?" my mom asked my dad in 2019 during one of their storytelling visits with the boys. "You are talking crazy."

"What are you talking about?" he responded, laughing. "*Stata zit* (shut up)."

The kitchen was their stage. They cooked together all the time.

"You are putting too much salt in the sauce," he would say. "And don't put too much salt. You always put too much salt."

"Don't tell me how to cook. You don't have to eat it."

"Well, good; my sauce is better anyway. I will make my own," he would say with a laugh. The kids would laugh.

My dad proposed to my mom in a letter in 1956.

"Before I came to America in 1954, your dad tried to give me a ring. I was fifteen. My dad told him and his dad, 'No. She is too young. We are going to America.'"

As we stand outside the church, my mom continues her story.

"So, his mom wrote a letter to her mom Anastasia, who was already in Frederick, and told Anastasia that I was moving to Frederick, that her son liked me, and to get to know me. And Anastasia did. We became very close. My mom was still in Cansano, so Anastasia became like a mom to me. She was a nice lady."

"What happened next?" I ask.

"Well, in 1956, your dad wrote a letter to his grandma Anastasia to give to my dad. The letter asked my dad for my address and permission to write me a letter. He told her yes. I think I still have the letter; I need to look. Well, then your dad started writing me and I wrote him back a few times, and he said he wanted to marry me. So, I wrote him back and said yes. It was different back then."

She continues. "But my dad didn't have any money to send me back to Cansano, so Anastasia gave me the money. My mom and sisters had just moved to Colorado in 1956, and my dad didn't have any money. So, Anastasia gave me the money. She was the nicest lady. Your dad bought my wedding dress. We got married in Cansano on March 28, 1957. None of my family were there. We had some relatives, some aunts, uncles, and cousins, but my mom and dad could not afford to come. And then we walked down this walkway to the piazza," she says, pointing down the steep walkway.

"Many people in the town came to watch the procession. That is the way we did it back then."

I wonder what it must have been like for her, all alone for her wedding day with no parents, siblings, or father to walk her down the aisle. I think about the procession to the church, which we just walked, the path to the piazza after the wedding, which I had unknowingly walked in the days before. I wonder if they had a reception with music and dancing. I wonder if they had confetti candy (sugar-coated almonds), which comes from Sulmona. We had visited Sulmona and the street of confetti shops the day before after our trip to Pescocostanzo and before the San Giovanni dinner.

As a child, I went to many Italian weddings of children of immigrants from Cansano and other towns in Abruzzo. There were many, it seemed—like three or four every spring and summer. The receptions were typically held in two places—for wealthier families, the grand ballroom on the Colorado School of Mines campus in Golden, Colorado, and for other families, the reception hall at the Moose Lodge in Longmont, Colorado. Aggie and I had our wedding reception at the Moose Lodge in 1990, with over eight hundred guests in attendance.

Every Italian, whether in Italy, the United States, Canada, or Australia, has celebrated major life events, like weddings, baptisms, and communions, with confetti from Sulmona. Confetti comes in every color, and I grew up looking forward to Italian weddings, where little lace bags of confetti are handed out to guests during the reception. Weddings also meant dancing to "La Tarantella" and Italian polkas like "Rosamunde." There was the money dance, where people lined up to dance with the bride and groom, and they pinned ten-, twenty-, fifty-, and one-hundred-dollar bills on the bride and groom. The bride and groom "made" thousands of dollars during the money dance. There was lots of food and wine and, of course, Italian wedding cookies. And there was confetti. It wasn't a real Italian wedding without confetti. My grandma Filomena was in charge of ordering them from Italy for the Ruscitti marriages and religious celebrations. Her other favorite sweet was torrone, a chewy nougat confection made of honey, sugar, toasted almonds, or pistachios that came in small, rectangular boxes with fancy fonts and flowers. Every Christmas, she ordered chocolate-, almond-, and orange-flavored torrone and gave some to each grandchild.

As we walked down a cobblestone side street the day before in Sulmona, we were overcome with the smell of almond and anise. Several confetti stores lined the streets, each selling their own special version of the candy and drawing many shoppers to the area. Outside of each store are old wine barrels filled with confetti in every color and displays with baskets of colored confetti shaped like flower arrangements. From a distance, they look real, but the colors are more vibrant. Many of the candied flowers have tiny confetti-shaped ladybugs.

We bought some bags of confetti and I was immediately transported back to my childhood and the weddings and family get-togethers. I loved those events.

TWENTY-SIX

The Sharp Dresser

My dad loved to gamble—poker, blackjack, and horse and dog racing—and argued that he had made much more money than he lost over the years and that he gambled to help the family, justifying his habit. But he actually was very good; he played in the World Series of Poker and the World Series of Blackjack and always seemed to win more than he lost. As a child I often went to dog and horse tracks with him, and as an adult we did several gambling trips to Las Vegas and Elko, Nevada. And he loved playing house card games with friends, especially during hunting trips.

The second Saturday in November of each year is opening day of pheasant hunting season in Colorado. Starting in the mid-2000s, my dad joined me and some of my friends, law partners, and clients to hunt pheasants. I grew up hunting with my dad and uncle, but we didn't hunt much in my twenties and thirties. I was too busy. And his eyes were not as good as they used to be, so his hunting skills had diminished. By 2010, it was no longer about the hunt—it was about hanging out with the guys. In the early years of our annual trip, we rented a bed-and-breakfast in Yuma, a small farming town in northeastern Colorado. After the couple that owned the B&B sold the home, we then stayed at the Nelson Inn, at best a two-star motel. The small town is so far east that the omnipresent Rocky Mountains with numerous peaks reaching fourteen thousand feet are no longer visible. When our group of ten or twelve city slickers descended into this plain country town each year, the locals definitely noticed. It is Mayberry, USA, and I always wondered if Sheriff Andy Taylor and Deputy Barney Fife would show up to check our hunting licenses.

The Friday night before opening day was an occasion that my dad most looked forward to. Every year, we would go to a local beer joint that serves steaks from the nearby farms. It is not steakhouse quality, but no one seems to care. The beer and whiskey are flowing, as are the stories about recent hunting and fishing trips.

And then after dinner, we would head back to the bed-and-breakfast or Nelson Inn for the main event: poker, dealer's choice. The stakes always started small, but before the game was over by around two a.m., we would have several pots over five hundred dollars. Not bad for a home game.

I remember one hunt in November 2010. My dad looked at his cards, his straw but stylish fedora sitting comfortably on his head. Everyone had a buzz, and a few of the guys were on their way to a serious hangover, making the next morning's five a.m. wake-up call and walk through dense cornfields in the cold Colorado fall morning uncomfortable at best. As we approached eleven p.m., we were playing strictly Texas hold'em. We were on the turn card, and the pot was close to three hundred already.

"Twenty dollars," said my colleague George Berg.

"Check."

"Check."

"Check."

"Bullshit. I can't get a fucking card. Fold," said Eric Kramer, a good friend of ours.

"Raise another twenty," boasted Justin, George's son and another one of my law partners.

"Check," I said.

"Fold."

It was my dad's bet. He chuckled, his eyes alive with the wonder of a child. He loved being one of the guys. He loved to gamble, and I had seen this move many times over the years.

"Justin, so you think you have me beat, eh young man?" he asked. "You better fold."

"Emilio, damnit, I have a great hand. Are you bluffing?"

My dad looked at Justin and laughed playfully. This was game play for my dad. Sometimes he was bluffing and sometimes he had the goods. You just never knew. "You are a bigga shotta lawyer, Justin. I want somma you money. You have lots, and I have a little. But I am telling you, I have you beat. You better fold." He laughed again and took a sip of some red wine.

"He is bluffing," said Derek, a local farmer who has become a friend and client of the firm. We would hunt his fields the next morning.

Several players folded, including me, and several, including Justin, stayed in. The river card (the last card of the hand) leads to more boasting, and the whiskey and wine lead to some aggressive betting.

He wasn't bluffing, and Dad won the pot.

"Damnit Emilio! You do that every time."

As I typically did, I went to bed earlier than anyone else, but my dad played for another hour or so and won over five hundred dollars for the night. He was one of the guys, and I suspected that even though they are my friends, clients, and work colleagues, they liked hanging out with him more. Over time, they would all become his friends, and he was a star on the trips.

The next morning, the sky was grey, and we could see our breath in the cold morning air. The morning came early for the late-night gamblers, and the smell of whiskey was pronounced in my truck as a group of five of us drove to the field. Our cavalry of trucks arrived at the first of several fields we would walk that morning, looking to harvest our limits. My dad and I were fine, but a few of the guys were hurting. My dad loved to have a good time, but I have seen him drunk only once or twice in my life.

Like an accordion, the large group sprawled across the cornfield. The corn had been harvested and the stalks had been cut, providing great cover for the pheasants. A few hunting dogs started running the corn rows hoping the flush the birds. Walking the fields was hard, as the stalks were difficult to traverse, super dense and thick in some areas. The ground was hard from the overnight freeze, and the mud tracks left by the farming equipment several weeks ago were now rock solid, providing more walking hazards. Other fields have equally thick brush, and sticker weeds are present everywhere. We would walk ten to fifteen miles that morning, stepping over and through the rough.

"Emilio, why don't you come and block with me and Larry?" asked George. Larry is another lawyer in Boulder and is in his mid-seventies, like my father. "My knees are bothering me, and we can catch up. We will get all of the birds they will miss."

They drove to the other end of the field to serve as blockers. Pheasants run on the ground and only fly if they feel threatened or sense something blocking their path. The blockers normally get the last shot at birds trying to escape.

The hunt was successful, and we harvested twenty-four pheasants. My dad plucked some of the more colorful feathers from the birds. "These will look good in my hats."

My dad was always a sharp dresser. When he wasn't working, he wore a button-up shirt, many times with a tie. My sisters' friends all thought he was handsome, and when my parents bought and operated their grocery store in the '80s and '90s, I would watch many women of all ages drawn to his charm, thick accent, and good looks. Even though he left Italy at age twenty-one, his accent remained strong. And he always wore a fedora. By the time he was fifty, his thick wavy hair had thinned and he was self-conscious about balding. So, he wore a hat each day, most times a fedora. He had tons of fedoras, one for each occasion. He wore straw fedoras when he was working in the yard or workshop, fishing, or hunting. He had felt fedoras for special occasions, like weddings or holidays. He had other hats for everyday wear. And he loved to enhance them with feathers he found in his yard or took off birds during our hunts.

"When we go to Italy, we need to buy more hats," he said before our 2013 trip.

My mom replied, "More hats?! You and those hats. You don't need anymore!"

"Be quiet, everyone loves my hats," he laughed.

^ ^ ^ ^ ^

Fast-forward from the hunting trip to the third day of our 2013 trip to Italy. After our visit to the church where my parents were married, we drive to Pacentro, a town that dates back to the eighth century and sits outside of Sulmona on the road to Cansano. The meadow below the town is filled with grape vines, nut trees, and olive groves. The village slowly climbs the side of the mountain, up and over several small hills and plateaus, creating a waterfall of homes and buildings along the side of the mountain, with three large towers from a medieval castle in the rear of the town. After several tight, twisting turns up the mountain, we park on a side street and enter the main piazza through an arch that connects two buildings. Several bars and cafés dot the piazza. Tuesday is market day in Pacentro, and tents line the small piazza with local vendors peddling fresh fruit and vegetables, clothing, purses and jewelry, and fine-crafted doilies, scarves, and hand towels.

"Wait until you see the market tomorrow in Sulmona. This is nothing," says my dad.

"When I was younger, we used to dress up real nice with a necktie all the time, and me and my friends Concetto and Donato would come here," he tells my son Donato and Izabella. "My dad bought me a suit for holidays, weddings, and funerals. I would dress up, and we pretended to be someone else. We had a lot of fun. We all had names; they called me doctor, and my friends, one was the lawyer and one the professor.

The people would look at us and say, 'Woah, look at these guys.' We would go to the bar and act like big shots. We were just teenagers."

He chuckles. "Those were good times." A mini lecture and teaching opportunity follows. "We had clean fun. Real fun. Not like the young people today, with all the drugs and drink, bad movies, computers, things that mess with your mind. Be smart, Grandpa," he says to Donato and Izabella.

My dad often spoke of his youth in contradictory ways: the misery, the poverty, the lacking, but also family, friends, music, and clean and simple times.

"Your grandpa, he looked good back then," my mom says.

"You did, too," he responds. "We are old now, not so good looking."

They laugh.

TWENTY-SEVEN

Fucking Cancer

It is April 20, 2017. I pick my parents up at five a.m. to take my dad to his testing at UC Health. He lives thirty minutes away, so I wake at up three thirty a.m. to have some coffee and shower. I try to do my morning routine of things I am grateful for, positive manifestations, and meditation, but I can't focus. Doctors, tests. This reminds me too much of Rina. Fucking cancer.

"I have lost another three pounds since last week," Dad says when he gets in the car. His voice is worried.

I don't answer. I know I should provide some positive assurance, but I don't know what to say and there is an awkward silence.

"What do you think about Rina's treatment?" he asks.

Before I can answer, my mom says, "*Dio mio*, I hope they can help her. We can't lose her." *Dio mio* means "Dear God."

I lie again. "She will be okay. She is seeing the best doctors in the world."

"I hope so," my dad says softly.

The rest of the car ride is quiet, each of us lost in thought. I am hoping for the best but am expecting the worst. My mom cannot handle losing her oldest daughter and her husband at the same time. I think of my sisters, Linda and Lora. I think of my children losing a grandparent, which would be their first.

The waiting room is filled with cancer patients at various stages of their diseases. They look sick. I avoid eye contact with the patients, hoping somehow to make this less real. The room is filled with characterless chairs and cheap art displaying flowers and mountain scenes. The room is cold, with people in the dying process. I stare down at the white tiles.

We don't wait long. "Emiliano Ruscitti," calls out the lady behind the counter. Crap, here we go.

We go back to a room with patient beds separated by curtains forming a U-shape around a central nurse's station. They ask my dad to undress and to put on a hospital gown. I step out to give him privacy. The room is sad, and I wonder how these people can do this job. I go back into his little area. Lying on the bed, he looks old and vulnerable. His legs are very thin and have almost no hair. I feel embarrassed to look at him. His once-thick chest and wide back look small as he lies in the bed. When did this happen?

After a few minutes, a series of doctors and nurses come by and ask numerous questions, some of which annoy me for some reason. "Do you consent to us trying to resuscitate you, if necessary?" one asks with no context.

"Is that possible?" my dad asks. "What would you do?"

"We have to ask this question." She then explains the process of resuscitation.

"Well, I don't want you to break my ribs or hurt me. If you can save me without doing that, then okay. Otherwise, no, I would rather die."

What? I think. This suddenly becomes very real. My mom squeezes Dad's hand. "Don't say that."

My dad patiently answers each question and old-man flirts with another one of the nurses. The doctor performing the scope comes in and explains the procedure in great detail. A scope will go down his throat with a small camera at the tip of a small needle-like instrument. They will take pictures in the bile duct and surrounding area, including his liver and pancreas. It will tell us what is causing the blockage. It may cause some irritation in the esophagus and throat. Depending on what they see, they may do a biopsy.

Bile ducts connect your liver to your gallbladder and small intestine and transfer nasty bile from your liver to your small intestine for processing.

"I am going to be OK, right doctor?"

"I have done thousands of these. You are in good hands."

"Thanks doctor; please take care of me."

"I will."

It is a long day. The procedure lasts several hours. I take my mom down to the cafeteria for coffee and then again later for a light lunch. My mom is nervous, and we have small talk. I bring my laptop and try to do some work. I realize I need to be more present for my mom and close my computer.

At 12:35 p.m., they call us into the room. He is awake but groggy. He tries to talk, but his throat hurts from the procedure. At 1:07 p.m., the doctor comes and has some images that he shows me. He explains what they found.

At 1:13 p.m., I text my sisters: "I have bad news."

TWENTY-EIGHT

1958

The immigrant's story is one of a generation having to suffer and work hard for those that follow. Usually, it is the first generation that suffers. My parents, like many Italian immigrants, took much of the pain and suffering for me and my sisters.

One Saturday morning in my childhood my father took me to work with him at Gardner Denver, a company he had worked for since the early '60s. I was about seven or eight at the time and very excited. This was my first trip to his normal place of work. On the way to Commerce City, an industrial suburb of Denver, we stopped to get donuts. The cashiers knew my dad.

"Emilio, how have you been?"

"Eh, working like a mule. Get my son a few donuts, whatever he wants. And a box of the old ones for the family."

I felt special. This rarely happened. We never went to restaurants, cafés, or donut shops. Many Saturdays my dad would come home from work with a box of day-old or two-day-old donuts. Never anything fresh. Today was different.

We got back in his white 1965 F-250 three-speed pickup truck, the truck I would learn to drive in a few years later. When we were young, all of us crammed into the cab of that old pickup, and I sat on the floor, with Rina, Linda, and my mom sitting in the bench-style seat next to my dad and Lora on my mom's lap. No seatbelts.

On the way to his work, my dad sang along to the old Italian songs playing on the eight-track player he had installed in the truck—classic songs by Domenico Modugno, Luciano Tajoli, and his favorite song, "Il Tuo Mondo," by Claudio Villa. I ate my donut. This was a good day.

"This is real music. Not the jungle music of today, with all that banging," Dad said.

We arrived at the factory. At the time, Gardner Denver manufactured industrial parts primarily for the oil and gas and energy industries. By the early '70s, my dad had become the lead pattern maker at the factory—using freehand measurement techniques, he created precise wood replicas of the object to be cast from the engineering specifications that were used to prepare the cavity into which molten material was poured during the casting process, a highly skilled craft that he learned on the job.

My dad's boss met us at the door.

"Who is this young man?"

"My son, Giovanni."

"Well let's put him to work," the boss said kiddingly.

"Giovanni, your dad is our hardest-working employee. He is the best. Learn from him."

"Oh, I don't want him to do this kind of work. Maybe a doctor, engineer, lawyer. A boss. Not this kinda work," he said.

Years later, I remember that day well. Perhaps this planted the seed. Or maybe it was my grandpa Panfilo telling me during the '70s, "You will be president someday." Maybe it was trying to escape the struggles of my family. But not going to college was never an option for me, and in 1989 I became the first person in my family on either side to graduate from college.

The grey plant was bleak and smelled of heavy chemicals that were new odors for me. My dad was the only worker on the shop floor that day. He was working on a special project for the boss man. I put on a hard hat and goggles and watched my dad do his work. Using hand cord measurement tools, he carefully took the paper designs and marked the piece of wood, which he then cut, using multiple tools, into a small mold. Sanding. Trimming. More cuts. More sanding. Measuring. Any error and the part could not be made to meet the design specs. How did he learn to do this? He only had a fifth grade education. I was not yet in fifth grade, I thought to myself.

Sawdust slowly filled the air, and a rich, almost exotic spice-like scent filled the room, overwhelming the chemical smells.

"We use mahogany wood," he told me. I don't know what that is and have never heard the word.

"It is a harder wood, better for the production process." The smell of the sawdust hung in the air, became comforting.

It took all day to make the pattern.

We took the metal stairs up to the third floor and went through a large wood door. We walked into his boss's office, which was filled with certificates and small plaques.

"I am done. Here it is."

"Emilio, this is amazing! This is important for the company. Thank you." The boss man shook my dad's hand, and I saw the mutual respect.

^ ^ ^ ^ ^

On the third day of our June 2013 trip, we return to Cansano in the early afternoon from our short excursion to Pacentro. Another multicourse lunch awaits. We tell my uncle about a little white dog that appeared out of nowhere as we entered a second, even smaller, piazza in Pacentro. The dog led us up a very steep stairwell to the one-thousand-year-old castle that was visible for miles. Several times, he stopped and turned to make sure we were all following him. After we toured the castle, the dog led us back into the center of town and then disappeared.

I tell my uncle that Aggie thinks it was a spirit guide.

"*Allora, è certo,*" he says in Italian. "Well, of course."

"Grandpa, can we go to the building where you went to school?" Donato asks.

"Yes, Grandpa, let's go."

We slowly walk through the town, which is quiet with the exception of a few birds singing their familiar tune and the deep buzzing sound of flies echoing from the park leading to the municipal building. The town is filled with flies, especially in this park. It is a hot June day and the air is thick; the old buildings smell of musty wood fires from decades ago and wet concrete from the humidity. We are sweating. After touring the municipal building, we walk down to an open area near the old fountain.

I recall a black-and-white photo of my dad at age twenty-one taken near the fountain below *La Partayova*. It sits on my credenza in my office, and I see it every day. But I can now place it. In the photo it is late January, early February 1958. My dad, who spoke and read no English at the time, is in a suit, tie, and heavy dark grey trench coat. He is stylish, especially his hair, which is short, and a small strand of hair hangs trendily over his left eye. He is surrounded by his brothers, his father, an uncle, and his mom. The men are all in suits. Zio Pietro wears sunglasses and a white suit. A large group of people are behind the family and around a car, which has an old travel trunk strapped to the top. They are sending my father off on his long journey to America. It looks like the whole village is sending him off. It was a big event when someone emigrated from Cansano. Some were envious. Others, like his brother Armando, had no desire to leave Cansano and the life they knew.

The trip to the United States started with a train ride south from Cansano where it connected with a larger train that took him to the port in Napoli. From there, he boarded the ocean liner *Saturnia*, which took him—and several hundred other Italian immigrants looking for a better life—across the Atlantic to Halifax, Nova Scotia, before arriving in New York on February 19, 1958. The trunk he traveled with carried everything he owned. Not quite the shirt on his back, but close. That trunk sat in my closet when I was a young boy. I often opened it and just stared inside. The inside had a satin liner and was decorated with an elegant design. Sometimes I thought about packing it and traveling the world like my dad.

My mom was waiting for Dad in Frederick, Colorado, having moved back to the United States after they married the year before on March 30,

1957. They had no honeymoon, only a few days and nights together in Cansano before she had to return to the United States. His grandparents on his mom's side were also in Frederick, as were a few other families that had emigrated from Cansano. Not much else was waiting. No job. No path to an education. No plans for learning English. With the exception of a few Ruscittis who remained in Cansano, the rest of his father's immediate family had immigrated to Australia.

CHAPTER TWENTY-NINE

The Wall Street Journal

My parents' struggles in the United States were different from their struggles in Cansano. After immigrating to the United States in 1954, my mom entered the American school system. With no ability to read or write English and only a few years of sporadic education in Cansano after the war, she—at age fifteen—and her friend Helen DiSalle were placed in a first grade class in Frederick elementary with six-year-olds. They were relentlessly teased and mocked.

"I don't want to go to school," Mom pleaded with my grandfather in Italian. "The kids are mean. I am embarrassed."

He agreed. "OK, you can leave school, but you will take care of the family until your mom can come. You will cook, clean, do laundry, and repair shoes and clothes."

My dad arrived in Frederick in 1958, then a small coal mining town with about a thousand residents. It looked nothing like Cansano. Located thirty miles north of downtown Denver and thirty miles east of the Colorado mountains, it was a vast expanse of nothing. The dirt road to town was flat and surrounded by prairie land, some of which was farmed for wheat and corn. Most of the homes were made of wood and had siding and asphalt shingle roofs, two things my father had never seen. Saying that the town lacked character was an extreme understatement. I wonder what my dad thought of Frederick when he arrived. It was barren compared to Cansano. No mountains. No fruit and nut trees. No grape vines or olive trees. No creeks. And I think to myself how hard it must have been to go to a foreign country and to have to start from the bottom. I wonder what he thought of the foreign land.

A family friend from Cansano helped Emiliano get his first job, working for the town at its water treatment plant and for a man named Frank Milavec.

"I started work with the city, one dollar and five an hour," he told Dante in 2018 during one of their many visits.

"Worked with Frank, a very nice guy. He helped me quite a bit, teached me the way things were done in America."

In the late '50s, early '60s, Dad went to night school with a few other Cansanese to learn beginner English. His assimilation was slow.

"We were the donkeys. We did the jobs no one wanted to do," he told me when I was young. "We were like the Mexicans are today. We did the real work. Not sitting behind some fancy desk."

"And many of the people, they didn't treat us right. 'Go back to your country, you wop,' they said. Or people would want to start a fight. Call me things like dago. I kept my head straight and stayed out of trouble. To hell with them, I thought. They were not better than me." (A wop is a racial slur for an Italian or a person of Italian heritage that means "WithOut Papers.")

I heard versions of this story my entire childhood.

"Remember, Juwaa, no one is better than you, but don't act like you are better than anyone either," he advised me often as a young boy.

After a few years of working for the town of Frederick, Dad worked on a pipeline project in Denver building ditches.

"I took any job I could get," he told Dante in 2018. His story, his words:

> I then went to work on road construction—the I-70 project in Denver—building bridges, paving the road. Western Paving Company. Then I got a job in construction building homes in

Boulder. And we used to drive together with my father-in-law, my uncles. It was me and him and his three brothers: Antonio, Rocco, and Augustine. Sometimes another brother, Felice, too. It was hard labor, cement, and we would help the carpenters and everything else.

We worked for Don, a very nice guy. He treated me great. When Rina was born, I took a week off. He paid me everything, treated me like a god. I never forgot that. That is how you treat people. Treat the smallest people like they are the biggest.

After that, I got a job for public service of Colorado, building new buildings. But a bunch of friends, some, they were working for Gardner Denver Company, which was producing all kinds of equipment for the mines, oil companies, mining companies, oil wells, and so on. So, I went to work there. At the same time, I was working two jobs, another company named Ebasco, building the plants for public service.

At night, I worked for Gardner Denver. In the day, doing construction for Ebasco. Sixteen-hour days, two full-time workdays, each day.

In the meantime, I also had a part-time job in Boulder. My boss there told me, 'Emiliano, when you want to work, you don't have to call. You come to work and you give me your time, and I pay you.'

I ended up saving $2,700 on a very minimum wage working day and night, seven days a week. I saved this money and called my mentor, the guy who owned the little four-room house we rented on Sixth Street in Frederick. I was paying forty dollars a month rent. That was more or less one [week's worth of work]. His name was Joe. He was a student, no mom, no dad—they both died. He was the owner of the house, and I asked him if he wanted to sell. I told him I didn't want to pay no more rent. I want to buy. He hesitated a little bit, and he called back the next day.

> 'I need the money,' he said. 'I want to go to college and be a doctor. If you want the house, I will sell it to you.'
>
> 'How much you want?'
>
> 'Three thousand dollars.'
>
> I said, 'Joe, I don't have that. I want to pay cash. I have $2,700. If you want to sell the house, I can give you that. I don't wanna pay no more rent.'"

Dad paused his story. He never used a credit card. Never.

"If you don't have the cash, don't buy it," he told me as a teenager and young adult. "The only time to borrow money is if you can make it work for you. Not for things. That is the American way. Make money work for you, not the other way around." To this day, I remember that every time I pull out a card to pay for something.

Dad continued with his story to Dante:

> Well, he sold it to me. The house was small, the family was growing. I made a nice home out of it. I had four more rooms in the house, and the house was big enough for the whole family. And I called for my dad in 1964 to move to America. I missed him, and I saw opportunity. He was a young man still. He came over here. But then he died of cancer in 1965. After only a year [in the United States].

^ ^ ^ ^ ^

My dad started smoking in 1965 when his dad died. "I was nervous and very upset I lost my father," he explained. "I was lost and they helped calm me."

From as early as I could remember, my dad was a heavy smoker. Two or three packs a day. Marlboro Lights. He smoked all the time, including in the house or car. When he was out, he would send me to Evezich's gas station to buy his smokes. It was a few blocks away, and I rode my bike or ran there. I was eight, nine, ten years old. They all knew me and knew my dad, as one of the Evezich brothers was married to a woman from Cansano. I could have been smoking them myself, but it was the '70s. People either didn't know of the danger or didn't care. Like seatbelts. Never wore one until I was in my twenties.

One spring day in 1978 when I was twelve, my dad and I were working in the garage. He started coughing uncontrollably—something that happened frequently. He started cursing. "These god damn fucking sons of bitches. They are making me sick. Juwaa, go get my carton of cigarettes in the house," he said angrily. I will never forget what happened next. Pack by pack, he tore them in half and threw the whole lot in the trash.

"I am never smoking those fucking things again."

And he didn't. Dad quit cold turkey after thirteen years of smoking several packs a day.

Back to his story that he shared with Dante:

> When I got the job for Gardner Denver, I started as a laborer at the heat treatment area. A very dirty job. My clothes were all black. Very dirty, and very, very hot. I worked there for a short time until I applied for a better job. I cleaned the executives' offices for a little while. Then I applied for a new job. I went to the straightening press [where] the steel comes off the furnace. I worked there and on the chrome plate press, and I worked very hard. The press was not that hard because I was quick. I had a good eye, and I had a touch. Nobody could beat me. I could do in one hour what they did in two days. Really. Then I got promoted again. I went to the assembly.
>
> But I got in a big argument with my boss [while I was] working the graveyard shift. He was coming to me and giving me trouble all the time. Finally, one morning, I went to the office and talked to the guy who hired me. I said, 'If you don't change me to a new

job—to the day shift—my boss is gonna end up in the bottom of the furnace. He is always bugging me.'

I was tough them days. Nobody bluffed me at the time, believe me.

My dad was tough and principled. In the early '70s, my dad took me to Gaetano's, an Italian restaurant in north Denver. Next to the restaurant was a market with the same name that sold imported Italian products. The shelves were stocked from floor to ceiling with pastas, flour for making pasta and bread, tomato sauces and pastes, olives, olive oil, balsamic vinegars, canned meats, canned sardines and anchovies, bottled *giardiniera* (pickled veggies), bottled peppers, biscotti, Italian cookies, and other products—all imported from Italy. In the rear of the store was a classic meat and cheese counter, with prosciutto, dried sausages, salami, and cheeses hanging from the ceiling. Crusty fresh bread sat in a basket near the counter, which was staffed by a loud, heavy-set older man with a white apron. The man sliced some mortadella and provolone and tore off the butt end of a baguette. "*Guaglione, mangia*," he said, handing me a small sandwich. "Young man, eat."

Another man came in from the back and greeted my dad. It seemed like they were friends. The man poured my dad a glass of wine. They talked for a few minutes, and my dad shopped. Later in life, as an adult, I learned that the restaurant and market were owned by the Smaldone crime family, the head of the Colorado underworld, and the restaurant was the crime family's headquarters.

When we left, Dad whispered to me quietly, almost under his breath, "You have to watch out for those people. They are *mafioso*. Be friends with them, respect them, and they will not bother you. But don't do what they do."

I listened intently. I was six or seven years old.

"When I came to America, they tried to get me to join. They got some other Cansanese to join. One of them went to jail. He has a scar on his face from here to here," Dad said, motioning from the corner of his mouth to his high cheek.

Many years later, I met the man with the scar and remembered this story. His mom was close friends with both of my grandmothers.

"One of the main bosses came to me one day," Dad said. "Maybe '63 or '64. He told me I could make a lot of money for the family by working for them. I needed the money, but I told him, 'Thank you for the opportunity, but all respect, no. This is not for me or my family. We will show you respect, but please don't bother me and my family ever again.' I was afraid, but I was very firm with him."

"They never asked me again. They respected me for saying no. You can't be afraid. Don't ever be afraid. You can do anything in this country."

He paused, perhaps for emphasis. "No one is better than you. Remember. Don't be afraid. You can do anything."

Decades later as an adult, I thought about the courage it took my father to stare down the mob boss and tell him no. My father, while certainly not perfect, always stood for what was right.

Back to the story he shared with Dante:

> The next morning, they switched me to the day shift. I eventually stopped working at Ebasco and stayed with Gardner Denver until 1982 when they were purchased by another company, Cooper Industries. The company [Gardner Denver] had a lot of trouble with unions. The company [Gardner Denver] started to lose some money because of the union. Gardner Denver told all of the employees at a big meeting—about two thousand people—'In a year's time, if you don't make this plant productive, we will lock the door. You will have no job no more.'
>
> So, when the day came and they closed the plant in Denver, and Gardner Denver was purchased by Cooper Industries, they offered me the job to move with them. I was one of a dozen left out of two thousand employees. It was the executives and me. They offered me to go on to West Virginia with them. I

was well liked. I decided not to do it. I had property, family and so on.

^ ^ ^ ^ ^

My family was, by any objective measure, poor. We had the basic necessities—food, a home, and clothing—but no luxury items. I was the kid who wore Dickies and shirts from Kmart, usually off the discount rack.

I remember one Christmas season very well. I don't remember the year. It was early December and we sat around the kitchen table. My dad cut open a pink plastic piggy bank that was in his bedroom. It had been there as long as I could remember. Coins spilled all over the table and onto the floor. We counted the coins as a family: $34.54.

My dad looked at my mom and said, in Italian, "That is what you have for Christmas this year. For the food, gifts. Everything. We cannot spend any more."

"*Va bene,*" she said. They were quiet.

That Christmas Eve, my dad started a new tradition. There was no Santa Claus. Christmas presents came from our parents, and we knew it. (We did, however, have *La Befana*, the Italian version of Santa Claus. She is the friendly witch of Christmas who rides a broomstick and brings candy, coins, treats, and small presents to "good" children on January sixth, the morning of Epiphany.) Our family opened gifts on Christmas Eve. No Christmas mornings running to the tree to see what Santa brought. That year, after our massive Feast of the Seven Fishes, which is a common Italian tradition, we sat around the tree and my dad took over. He grabbed each present and made a production of each gift.

"What is this?" he laughed as he grabbed a present.

Shaking the box, he said, "Is this rocks? Or coal? Did Linda get a box of rocks? What did you do this year to deserve this?" he laughed louder.

We all laughed and the production went on for a few minutes.

"Or is it a dress? Or a doll?"

By the time we opened the gift, the anticipation was building and it didn't really matter what was in the box. We didn't care. Maybe this was his way of hiding the fact that he couldn't give us what he wanted to. But Christmas Eve was memorable that first year, and we continued this tradition every year since, even when my parents had nine grandchildren. It took hours to open presents.

Dad put on a show for his adult children too, even when we no longer received gifts but, rather, just a card with a check. "What is in this envelope? Doesn't sound like money. A bill? Lora, this is a bill. You owe me money." He laughed as he handed the card to Lora. Inside was a check for a few thousand dollars.

And the check *always* spelled the in-laws' names wrong. Aggie was "Aggy" or "Aggi" or "Agee." We couldn't wait to see how it was spelled every year.

While working at Gardner Denver in the late 1960s and early '70s, Dad started taking home the *Wall Street Journal* from the executives' offices. His spoken English was broken but getting slightly better. But he could not read or write well. I don't know how it came to be—or why—that he took home the *Journal*, but it taught him to read and write English. And it taught him about business and financing. By the mid-1970s he was investing in real estate and had just started his construction company with his brother Luciano. He slowly started buying old homes in Frederick, renovating them and renting them out. He dragged me along to each renovation project, and I handed him the tools he asked for and helped when I could, which is to say probably not as much as I thought I was doing at the time. As evidenced by the fact that, today, I hire a handyman for any project in my house.

"You be a lawyer, and I will handle everything else," Aggie often tells me. I laugh.

"But I used to build houses with my dad. Seriously."

"And, by the way, it is called *competitive advantage*," I say to her. "I *choose* to hire people to do this. I can make more money being a lawyer—something I am good at—and hire someone else to do that stuff that they are better at. That makes the economy work and stay in balance."

"Riiiight," she says.

By the time I was in high school, my dad owned three or four homes in Frederick. At the same time, he and his brother Luciano bought vacant land in Frederick and neighboring Longmont and built homes on weekends and after work. Each year, they built a home or two. On many Saturday mornings, he dressed up and took me to the United Bank of Longmont, and I listened as he talked to his lender about loans he needed for the projects.

One Saturday, we took a bottle of my dad's homemade wine and some homemade prosciutto and fresh sausage to the lender, who had been to the house for dinner in the past.

"Emilio, anything you need," the banker said to my dad after they talked about a loan.

In the car, my dad explained that he obtained a signature loan—no collateral, no financial statements, no business plan. Just his signature on a loan for a new construction project. "If you keep your promises and treat people right, they will take care of you."

In 1983, after turning down the transfer to West Virginia, Dad opened Sunrise Market with my mom and sister Rina in Berthoud, a sleepy town filled with large maple and ash trees about twenty miles north of Frederick. He knew nothing about running a grocery store, and it became a family business where we all worked, mostly for free. Rina did the ordering and ran the books. My dad did what he did best—he negotiated for the best prices from vendors. And he loved going to the local farms and buying fresh, in-season produce in the same way he learned to negotiate in Sulmona.

"How much for the corn?" he asked Mr. Tanaka, a local farmer. This conversation could have happened—and did happen—any year between 1983 and 1998, with Mr. Tanaka and every local corn, tomato, potato, cucumber, radish, spinach, cabbage, lettuce, cantaloupe, peach, and watermelon farmer in the area. I often tagged along. For me, it was a workout opportunity. While my football teammates were working out in the gym and getting ready for two-a-days, I was working at the store. For free. Football season was about to start, and I had to stay in shape. I did push-ups and pull-ups anywhere in the store when I had a free second, and loading and unloading the truck was a way to stay in shape.

"Six corn on the cob for a dollar," Mr. Tanaka would negotiate.

"That is too much."

"That is the price."

"What if I bought the whole truckload?" my dad asked, pointing to his 1965 F-250.

A few minutes later, the deal was made and I got my workout in, loading the truck.

We parked the old white pickup truck on the sidewalk in front of the store. The beat-up truck parked in front of the store was a good sign for customers. It meant we were running a special: "Twelve corn on the cob for $1." The corn sold out in a few hours.

We did this all summer for almost every fruit and vegetable that came into season—tomatoes, Colorado peaches, apricots, watermelons, cantaloupe, and other vegetables and fruits filled the back of the old pickup truck. On September 13, 1994, Alicia Lynch, a reporter with the *Longmont Daily Times-Call*, wrote an article about my parents, the store, their food, and the old pickup truck:

> In Berthoud, good home cookin' is as close as the corner store.
>
> The Sunrise Market, 357 Mountain Avenue, has served the community for more than thirty years. For the past eleven, it has been operated by Emiliano Ruscitti of Frederick.
>
> Together with his wife Maria and their daughter, Rina, the Italian family has transformed the market into a community fixture featuring locally grown produce—in season—and award-winning spaghetti sauce, meatballs and sausage.

. . .

Summer and fall, Ruscitti's battered Ford pickup sits in front of the store, its bed alternately filled with corn, watermelons or other produce from local farmers.

'I make a special trip each morning to bring it in' Ruscitti said. 'Our produce is vine ripened. If I sell a tomato, it's gotta taste like a tomato.'

. . .

While compact, the store does include four double aisles, a butcher shop, storage area and family kitchen where the Ruscittis and their employees gather.

The homey kitchen is also where Maria presides, daily making her spaghetti sauce which is bottled and sold exclusively from the store.

. . .

'I love to cook,' Maria Ruscitti said. 'I started the sauce by just cooking for us, then people came in the store and smelled it and I gave them a taste. They said, 'Why don't you sell it?'

And sell she has. The bottles contain the Ruscittis' private label featuring a picture of the main plaza in their hometown of Cansano, Italy, located near Rome. The label also contains the Ruscittis' take of journeying to America as teenagers with their families.

^ ^ ^ ^ ^

The *Journal* also taught Dad about stocks, and by the late '70s, he started buying stock. It started with small amounts at first. It wasn't until much later that I realized how good of a trader he was. But I should have known. The then-twenty-one-year-old man who came to the United States with little more than the shirt on his back, and who could speak no English, had no skills or proper training, and completed only a fifth grade education in Italy, sold Sunrise Market and retired at age sixty-two.

Sixty-two. Most Americans have to work into their seventies. And they graduate from college in the United States.

Back to our walk on the June 2013 afternoon. We enter *La Partayova*, and fortunately the buildings provide a brief respite from the afternoon heat as we climb up the staircase through the ruins. The picture of my dad leaving Cansano remains in my head. We return to our rooms and collapse for a short nap. The night would bring another big meal and a nighttime walk to the piazza.

I could get used to this.

CHAPTER THIRTY

Coffee with Zio Pietro

June 26, 2013—a Wednesday—is market, or *mercato*, day in Sulmona. My dad was *so* excited for this day. He had been talking about it the entire trip. As usual, I wake up before Aggie and quietly dress and leave the room. I look for my dad but don't see him, so I walk down the driveway and go downstairs to the kitchen to make myself an espresso. Zio Pietro enters the room.

"Good morning, nephew. You are up early," he says cheerfully in Italian.

"Yes, no matter where I am, I wake up around four thirty or five a.m." My Italian is better but choppy and hesitant.

"Me too. Let's go to my house, and we will talk and have a coffee and biscotti."

His home is across the driveway. It is a large building with five separate apartments. He lives alone on the second floor. His first wife died of cancer in the '80s, and he remarried a much younger woman from Russia who lived in Milan, a six-hour drive from Cansano, with her mother and sister. Pietro was in his seventies when they married, she in her thirties. This caused much scandal in the family.

Things I heard from family in America: "Why is he with her? She is so much younger than him."

"She is a gold digger. She wants his money and property."

She came to visit Pietro once a month, and while he wanted more, he seemed to be happy and content with the arrangement.

My cousin Panfilo owns the apartment on the first floor, but he lives in Sulmona with his wife. The third floor apartments are vacant, and my uncle occasionally rents them out to visitors from the United States and Canada. My cousin Rocco owns one of the two apartments on the second floor, which he lives in mostly alone, as his wife and two daughters live in northern Abruzzo with her mother. This is another strange family arrangement, but one that I learn is fairly common in Italy. Many adults care for their aging parents in Italy. Retirement homes are unheard of, and it is sacrilegious to put a loved one in a home with strangers. So, Rocco's wife is caring for her aging mother, and they visit Cansano every few weeks. The rest of the time he lives alone.

My uncle's apartment is quaint and clean. I never knew her, but I feel the presence of his first wife, Ida. The home is still decorated in her style and with her furniture from the '70s. The kitchen is small by American standards, resembling a small New York studio apartment. Pietro starts brewing the espresso in an old-fashioned and worn-out stovetop moka espresso pot and boils milk in a small pot. The room quickly fills with the aroma of cedar and pepper with a touch of toasted nuts. The milk comes to a boil, and with the moka pot in one hand and the milk pot in the other, he blends each cup with half espresso and half milk with the touch of an experienced barista. On his small table sits some biscotti, including a few gluten-free biscotti he picked up for me. The biscotti makes a cracking sound as I break it in half for dipping into the espresso. A few crumbs fly in the air and the smell of anise and vanilla dusts the room.

I dip the hard biscotti into my coffee. As it softens, it brings back another memory. As a child, I spent a lot of time with Grandpa Panfilo and Grandma Nunziata, my mom's parents. After my grandpa died of lung cancer in 1982, I spent nights at my grandmother's house, as she was afraid to be alone. Nunziata was a dipper. She made me *latte and caffè*, a cereal bowl of hot Italian coffee, steamed milk, and several teaspoons of sugar. Sometimes, she gave me a plate of Italian cookies, Stella Dora cookies, or biscotti, which are all hard and made for dipping. Sometimes she toasted day-old bread and tore the bread into chunks and put them in the latte and café. "*Mangia*," she would say. "*Vuoi di più*? (Do you want more?)" And before I could answer, more cookies or pizzelles were on my plate. There was no saying no.

The coffee and cookie this morning are the best I have ever had—or so it seems. Everything tastes and smells better here. Coffee and cookies with my Zio became my morning routine in my future visits. In 2017, I returned to Cansano for the first time without my parents. In 2019, Aggie and I returned to Cansano without any of our children. During those visits, I spent a lot of time with my zio. We both looked forward to our morning café and biscotti, and as I became more comfortable with my Italian, we became close. He confided in me about his second wife and how strange it was that she lived so far away. We talked politics, business, and lawyering in America.

Pietro stands. "*Allora, devo andare a lavorare. E oggi vi porto tutti al mercato di Sulmona*," he says. "I need to go to work. And I will take all of you to the market in Sulmona today."

After he leaves, I walk up the driveway and wait around a few minutes to see if my dad will come out to join me. I don't knock on the door as I don't want to wake my mom up if she is sleeping. After a few more minutes, I assume he is sleeping, and I walk down *Via Roma* and again explore the small town. On each walk I see something different: shutters hanging delicately on windows threatening to fall with the next strong wind; decaying doors with magnificent metal ring-shaped door handles on some, and missing on others (taken by visitors wanting to savor a memory from their ancestral homes); and beautiful ornamental edging on decrepit balconies and rooftops. Every few homes, I see new wood shutters, fresh terra-cotta stucco, and clay pots filled with colorful flowers hanging on balconies—evidence of life in those homes. Some areas have three to four remodeled homes in a row.

A small, thin dog that I have seen a few times during the trip approaches me. She is knee high and has a golden coat of short hair. She is very friendly and joins me for my walk, running ahead of me at times and stopping to make sure I am following. I think back to the spirit guide small dog the day before in Pacentro.

The distinctive smell of the town is now familiar and comforting. No one is out; with the exception of the birds chirping, the town is silent. I walk through streets I have yet to explore—*Via Umberto, Via Umberto II*. Some streets and alleys with no names. I wonder who lived in the homes then and now. Were their stories like those of my family? But mostly—and for the first time in many years—my mind is still. Silenced are the constant tangled thoughts of family challenges, never-ending work deadlines, legal arguments to make, contracts to draft, difficult opposing counsel and clients to manage, and office management and cultural issues that sometimes strangle and paralyze me. I am in the moment, a form of walking meditation before I had ever heard the phrase—and which I would later work hard at replicating back home.

Before I know it, an hour has passed and the stray dog and I are back at Rocco's bed-and-breakfast. Rocco is outside, having just returned from helping his father make ricotta cheese. This was his morning routine. He woke up early to make the ricotta and then worked all day in his two pharmacies. "You have met Luna," he says in Italian. "She is the town dog. She belongs to everyone."

During all of our return trips to Cansano, Luna became my constant companion on my morning walks and came to the bed-and-breakfast almost nightly to be fed by Aggie. It was almost like she remembered us. Perhaps she did.

By now, Aggie is up, doing yoga while facing a large, open window with the mountains in the distance. The aroma of burning wood from the fireplace in the home next door lingers in the air.

"I love this view and smell," she says.

"I know. I love this town. I am starting to understand the romance my dad and all the other Cansanese have with this place."

"I am not moving here," she says.

"I know. We can buy a place and visit every year. I like it here."

"We will see."

CHAPTER THIRTY-ONE

Overwhelmed

April 20, 2017. My text to my sisters continues:

> They found cancer in the lower bile duct. They need to wait for the results of the biopsy, which will be in seven to ten days. They don't think he is a candidate for surgery because of his age and heart, but we need to get him to a surgeon. Chemotherapy is an option. Really overwhelmed right now.

After a few responses from my sisters, I send one more:

"Mom is crying and dad is worried."

CHAPTER THIRTY-TWO

Bocce

Today, market day, is our last full day in Cansano. Tomorrow we will take the train to Rome for a few days and then another train to Naples where a car will pick us up and take us to the Amalfi Coast, where we will spend the last few days of our trip. *Piazza Garibaldi* is the main square of Sulmona and is located in the shadow of the thirteenth-century aqueduct. A baroque fountain sits in the middle of the square, and the road loops around the rectangular piazza like a racetrack. The aqueduct lines one side of the piazza and the other three sides are lined with trees; bottegas, cafés, and restaurants fill the first level of the buildings with apartments on top. On Monday, Tuesday, Thursday, Friday, and Sunday, the piazza is relatively quiet, with locals crossing the piazza and, depending on the time of day, sitting at the tables having coffee, wine, an Italian beer, or an Aperol Spritz.

But on Wednesdays, like on Saturdays, the piazza is a sea of white tents, tables, and food vans. Today is the *mercato* in Sulmona. Almost every town and city in Italy has at least one neighborhood market day, a tradition as old as the cities themselves. Some markets are only food markets, specializing in baked goods like bread and pastries, local produce, dry pastas, meats and cheeses, or seafood (especially in the coastal towns). Many sell household goods, most featuring beautiful linens. Some sell clothing, shoes, and jackets. Others are artisan markets. Many sell ornaments, toys, and antiques. And some sell jewelry and leather products, like purses. The *mercato* is an important part of the economy for many towns, bringing in tourists and shoppers from neighboring towns, many of whom will also shop in the local bottegas or grab lunch or a coffee, beer, or wine in the local restaurants. Many locals sell their fresh produce, cheeses, or meats. And while towns have small grocery stores, locals rely on the market for food, especially fresh produce. The locals arrive early for the best produce and fresh bread, and then return late for the bargains, when the food products must go or they will spoil.

The market is also a cultural event. Italians are social and the market is another opportunity to talk, eat, and drink. And bargain. Bargaining is allowed, if not expected.

The market in Sulmona sells everything and the piazza is packed when we arrive. We arrive late, so the market is in full swing.

Pockets of older men and women catch up on the streets around the market, carrying bags filled with fresh food items. Some of the older men are dressed up in suits, ties, and fedoras, and the older women are in dresses. Professionals come in and out of offices, grabbing a morning espresso at the bars that line the streets. They don't seem to be burdened by time like Americans.

As I watch, I am struck by how communal Italians are. Everyone is engaged in conversation—with passion. Many of the locals likely talked to each other the night before during the *passeggiata*. What were they talking about? What was new or different from the night before? People seem more interested in the lives of their neighbors here in this village than they seem back home. Why don't Americans talk to each other more? We are so busy, but this seems like a better way to live. The pace is different here.

The piazza center is filled with shoppers going from vendor to vendor. The food vans and tents selling food to order sit on the outside of the market with the bakeries nearby. The vendors dish out pork sandwiches, sausage and peppers, panini with fresh cold cuts and cheeses, roasted chickens, arancini balls, local lamb dishes, fresh pasta dishes, and other local specialties. The aromas are tantalizing, even if you are not hungry.

Dozens of produce vans and tables line the exterior of the market, selling every possible seasonal vegetable and fruit. This is truly farm-to-table, and likely the inspiration for the farmers' markets back home. There is no reason to shop for produce in grocery stores with the abundance of fresh produce in these markets, especially for towns like Sulmona that have two weekly markets. Prices are displayed on handwritten placards. But those are just a suggestion.

I watch my dad go to work.

As we go from table to table, he carefully examines the produce, picking some up to test for firmness and smelling others.

"*Quanto per un chilogrammo*?" my dad asks. "How much a kilogram?"

"*È scritto sulla carta*," responds the vendor. "It is written on the card."

"I will give you five euro," my dad says in Italian, offering roughly half the price.

This plays out over and over, sometimes with success, sometimes not. We buy melons, apricots, cherries, Italian lettuces, peas, tomatoes, zucchini, and nuts. We buy enough for a week, even though we are leaving Cansano for Rome tomorrow morning. My dad always bought in bulk, his garage filled with cases of different in-season produce, cans of tomatoes, and jars of olives, pickled vegetables, and other items. "You get better prices," he tells me often.

"But you don't need a case of cherries. You can't eat them all."

"I give them away." And he did.

It was not uncommon for him to call and say something like, "I bought a case of ribeye steaks and two cases of tomatoes. Do you need any?"

"No, dad, we just went shopping yesterday. We are good."

"OK, well, if you need any, let me know."

After shopping for produce, we walk through the center of the market and buy a few items, including a stovetop moka espresso pot. My dad continues his bargaining. He sees a set of bocce balls and starts the negotiation. He doesn't need bocce balls, as he has several sets back home, including a set from the 1970s that meant a lot to him. Besides, we have no room in our luggage for the balls. But it doesn't matter. For him, negotiating was a game, a competition, and he loved being in that moment. Several things brought him pure joy and contentment—playing cards, the *mercato*, the stock market, and playing bocce.

One warm fall weekend in 1978 we went to a park in Denver for a large bocce tournament. Bocce is an ancient game that started during the Roman empire, with teams of two, three, or four players playing on soil or clay courts. Tournament play is usually four players per side. The object is for a team to get the highest number of bocce balls as close as possible to the *pallino*, a small white ball that is thrown at the beginning of each frame from one end of the court to the other. The scoring team receives a point for each of their balls that is closer to the pallino than the closest ball of the other team. The scoring team throws the pallino to start the next frame, and games go until eleven points are earned. Each player throws two bocce balls of the same color. Teams have openers—players that are good at getting the ball close to the pallino to open a frame—and players good at knocking out opening teams' balls that are close to the pallino. My dad was a master at knocking out opponents' balls, so he was always the last to throw.

I had attended bocce tournaments in Colorado with my dad and grandfather Panfilo for years. The Sons of Italy, a group of Italian Americans, hosted tournaments throughout the summer and fall. Teams usually played in single-elimination brackets, and by the evening a champion was crowned. Larger tournaments were double elimination. Most events were held at the Sons of Italy club in Arvada, a suburb of Denver with a heavy Italian American population. Immigrants from different regions like Piemonte, Emilia-Romagna, Umbria, Lazio, Molise, Campania, Calabria, and Abruzzo played most weekends. Winning was a source of pride for the players and their communities. The differences between the groups were obvious to me, even as a young boy, and I loved watching the competition and the interactions. The men from north Denver, mostly immigrants from southern Italian provinces like Campania and Calabria, were loud and gaudy. They wore wife-beater T-shirts and drank heavily all day. They reminded me of bowlers. The men from western Denver suburbs like

Arvada and Golden were from northern Italian provinces like Piemonte and Emilia-Romagna and seemed more refined to me, students of the game. Maybe like golfers. They dressed better. Long-sleeve button-ups, slacks, and fedoras. And the men from the mountain provinces like Abruzzo and Molise lived in Frederick and parts of central Denver. They were the grinders—the outdoorsmen, hunters, and fishermen.

The games got heated. One such incident:

"*Siamo più vicini*," yelled one man to my dad's team. "We are closer."

"*Porca la miseria. Sei cieco*," responded my dad. "Holy shit, are you blind?"

"*Ah, vaffanculo! È il nostro punto*," said the opponent. "Oh, fuck you. It is our point."

Someone pulled out a tape measure and measured who was closer and called the point for my dad's team. This did not resolve the dispute.

"*Hai spostato la palla. Ah, fanculo*," yelled the man. "You moved the ball. Ah, fuck!"

It seemed like the yelling would end with a fight. It never did, but this carried on all day in most matches—in every tournament I went to.

But, by nighttime, most arguments were forgotten. And the best part of the tournaments, it seemed, was the dinner that followed. Wives and many children arrived after the tournaments were done, and Italian polkas, folk songs, and *stornelli* (simple Italian street songs) filled the air. Pots of food filled several tables: grilled Italian sausage meatballs (some in marinara sauce and some not), aluminum containers with rigatoni and spaghetti in marinara sauce, bowls of salads, baskets of crusty rolls, and plates of pizzelle and hard cookies. On another table were jugs of Carlo Rossi wines served in small plastic glasses. There was laughing, dancing, singing, drinking, and eating. The rivalries were gone, and it was a big community, much like I saw later on my trips to Italy.

But this was a big tournament in the fall of 1978, with around eighty teams participating. It was the biggest gathering I had seen. The winner would advance to represent Colorado in the first-ever US National Bocce Championship in 1979 in Las Vegas. My dad's team, named L'Aquila, which means Eagle, was made up of Carmine DeSantis, John DiGregorio, Tommy Villani, and Emilio DiGiallonardo, who was the alternate. They were all from Cansano. The tournament, played over two days, was double-elimination. My dad's team won, advancing to the national championship. Which they also won. My dad and his teammates were the national champions of the first-ever US National Bocce Championship. Their victory was reported by sportswriter Sam Cook in the *Longmont Times-Call*:

> There is a decaying old ballfield in this sleepy little Italian community with a clay infield as dry and hard as the pavement of Interstate 25. It's the kind of surface that sends neighborhood sandlot baseball players home with strawberries on their hips when they try to stretch a single into a double. Pete Rose wouldn't be caught dead in mid-air above this unforgiving surface in one of his patented hair-a-flying, headfirst dives.
>
> Across the street from this parched baseball diamond live two Italian gentlemen, John DiGregorio and Carmine DeSantis, who find the infield just to their liking. They don't run and they don't slide, so they don't come home with skin missing from their hips. In fact, they don't even play baseball, the great American pastime.
>
> No, they use the smooth, hardpacked surface of that dilapidated infield to play the great Italian pastime: bocce ball. So well do they play this unusual sport that, together with their friend Emiliano Ruscitti of Frederick and a couple of other bocce ball experts from Denver, they brought home gold medals from the recent International Federation of Bocce Ball National Tournament in Las Vegas.
>
> In two days of competition, the Frederick team won three of four games against teams from California, Arizona and Nevada, and won the championship on the basis of most cumulative points. They won twice on the first day, beating an Arizona team and a team from San Francisco which boasted a club membership

of more than 400. The Frederick club, by contrast has just six members. On the second day, they won their opening game with a team from Nevada, then fell to the same San Francisco team they had beaten the day earlier.

"The last game everyone was tired," explained the fifty-one-year-old DeSantis, chewing on his ever-present cigar.

Two regular members of the Frederick team, Tom Villani and Emilio DiGiallonardo, were unable to make the trip. They were replaced by Joe Asciutto and Frank Busnardo of Denver.

The Frederick team, name Aquila after the Italian province where each of the Frederick residents was born, found play in Las Vegas a far cry from its home court at the baseball diamond.

"Their courts were of fine sand on top of blacktop," said DeSantis. "Dirt is a lot slower."

But that wasn't all that was different.

"They were real strict," said Ruscitti, forty-two. "You couldn't drink or smoke while you were played, and you had to ask permission to leave."

Asked if that cramped the Aquila team's style at all, DeSantis replied quickly, "Oh yeah. Here we have a drink, we smoke . . . I caught hell three or four times out there.

"But it was beautiful. I'd do it again next weekend."

By winning in Las Vegas, the Frederick team qualified to compete in the upcoming international tournament in Australia. But it's doubtful Aquila will make that trip. "It takes times and a lot of money," said Ruscitti.

Bocce ball (pronounced "botch-a-ball") is gaining in popularity, said the fifty-five-year-old DiGregorio, especially in the west. Some 200–300 persons were on hand to watch the competition in Las Vegas. The Aquila team members were especially pleased that a Las Vegas television station put together a ten-minute feature on the sport during the tourney, and that a Las Vegas newspaper devoted an entire photo essay to the unique game.

Bocce ball is played on a rectangular court similar in size to a shuffleboard court. A small ball called a pallino, about the size of a golf ball, is rolled from one end of the court toward the other end. Each team member has two metal bocce balls, similar in size to croquet balls but heavier. Points are earned by lagging the bocces nearer the pallino than the other team does, or by throwing the bocces at opponents' bocces and knocking them out of the way.

"It is a good game for old timers, young, all ages," said Ruscitti. "People 70, 80 years old can play. It is good exercise for them. It shows them they can still do something. It makes them feel good."

The Frederick team plans to hold a tournament at the ballfield in September. With local rules in effect, DeSantis should be able to make it through the day without "catching hell."

"We'll have some drinks, some food and a little dancing at the end," he said, flicking the ashes off his cigar stylishly.

It ought to be a gala day at the old Frederick ballfield.

^ ^ ^ ^ ^

A celebration of the team's achievements did eventually come. In February 2019, the town of Frederick honored the team by constructing two bocce courts in Miner's Park and dedicating the courts to the team. John and Tommy had already passed away, and Carmine, Emilio, and my father were very sick. Carmine and my dad planned to attend the ceremony. They had not talked in decades due to a silly argument that separated a lifelong friendship. Carmine and his wife lived a block away from us when I was child, and they were also my godparents (as well as Rina's and Linda's)—a big deal in Italian culture. Our families were always together when I was young. In the weeks leading up to the ceremony, I urged my dad talk to Carmine.

"What do I say to him?"

"Tell him you are sorry for your role in what happened."

"I don't want to do that. He was wrong."

"I am sure you were wrong too. Dad, forgiveness is freedom. You are both old men. You are both sick. Put it behind you."

"You are right. I will talk to him."

At the ceremony, I stood next to my dad. I saw Carmine come to the park. He was in a wheelchair and looked very aged. Everyone in attendance knew about their disagreement, and everyone wondered what would happen. The argument was stupid, but they were hardheaded Italian men.

Carmine approached and got out of his wheelchair. Struggling to stand, he grabbed my dad's hand.

"*Compare*," he said. "*Compare*" means godfather. "I am sorry. I was wrong."

"I am sorry, too," my dad responded. They embraced and talked for ten to fifteen minutes about the life that had passed them both by.

I was proud of my dad. This should have happened long ago. After the dedication, they played a game of bocce together, shadows of their younger selves. They laughed and promised to see each other more.

^ ^ ^ ^ ^

Back to Sulmona: my dad tells the vendor about the bocce championship, hoping this will get him a better price. It doesn't, and we leave the market without bocce balls that he doesn't need.

CHAPTER THIRTY-THREE

The River

It is May 5, 2017. A Friday. I take my dad fly-fishing on a private fishing ranch on South Boulder Creek with two miles of blue-ribbon private river—the best fishing Colorado has to offer. I booked the outing the day after learning about his diagnosis in April. I wanted to spend time with him and create memories. We don't talk about the diagnosis on the drive up to the river. It is a beautiful spring Colorado day without a cloud in the sky. As we drive through the mountains west of Boulder to the ranch, I think about my childhood fishing trips with my dad. Our roles have since reversed. I think about Cansano. The Colorado mountains are beautiful, but there is something about the mountains in Abruzzo that captivated and almost possessed me. I miss Cansano. Over the years, we were fortunate to take several trips to Cansano—one in 2013, one in 2014, and one planned for later in 2017. My dad is debating whether to come on the 2017 trip. "This will probably be the last time I can go."

The diagnosis weighs heavy on all our minds. Bile duct cancer is rare and hard to treat. And the prognosis is not good for most people. Six months. A year. Two years at most, the doctor tells me privately during Dad's latest appointment in April. Outwardly, I suggest to my dad that we talk to the doctor to get his advice. I was working on getting him in to see a specialist at MD Anderson in Houston. Inwardly, I knew Dad was right. I wondered if it was even safe for him to go at all.

I force my concerns from my head. Today, we fish. Today is a day we live for. It was gorgeous out, I had taken a day off work, and I was fishing with my dad.

We are only two weeks out from Dad's endoscopy and stent procedure, and he is pretty weak and still losing weight. No decisions have been made on his treatment. The doctors want him to get stronger. The guide helps him set up the rod with two flies, as his hands are not steady. We walk, slowly, up the river and after the short ten-minute walk, my dad has already invited the guide over for wine and dinner.

We stop, and the guide tells him where to cast. "I don't want to go into the river," Dad says. "They tell me I have this damn cancer, and I am not strong."

"That is OK," says the guide. "You can fish from the bank."

"I am sorry," my dad says, apologizing for his condition as if he were letting the guide down.

I see a side of my father I had never seen. Vulnerable.

Within minutes, he lands a twenty-four-inch German brown trout.

"That is the biggest brown trout I have ever caught," he tells the guide. He sounds like a little boy. He smiles wide while holding the fish for a picture.

"You are about to catch many more," the guide said.

After a few hours, it is lunch time, and we head back to the lodge. I mostly watch, helping my dad and hoping he is having a good time. "I will see you after lunch," the guide says. "We have three or four more hours of fishing to do."

My dad invites the guide to lunch.

We walk into the lodge. It is a rustic mountain lodge with oversize timber beams running across the ceiling. My dad stumbles a bit, and I help balance him. "I think I am done for the day," he says. They bring us a catered lunch, but I had packed some wine and my dad brought his homemade prosciutto and some provolone cheese. We share with the guide. We sit on the patio by the rushing river. We talk and laugh. And the man we had just met became my dad's best friend.

It was a nice day.

^ ^ ^ ^ ^

The next day, Saturday, May 6, 2017, I am running our annual all-partner meeting, where we review financials, determine associate raises, and make other business decisions. In years past, the event was boring, not inspiring, and oftentimes contentious. It is my second year as managing partner of the firm, and I have spent over forty hours getting ready for the meeting. Most law firms are not run like traditional businesses. The same was true for our firm. However, having represented many companies and attended countless board meetings, I was determined to change our culture and run our law firm more like a corporation.

My agenda for the day was not unlike what I had seen my clients do. I wanted to set objectives for the next twelve to eighteen months. I wanted to discuss succession planning. These were things we never discussed. I wanted people to leave inspired and ready to take the firm to the next level. I have ice breakers planned for the beginning and an inspirational speaker to set the tone for the day and to inspire people. The ice breaker is a success, and the room is relaxed. The speaker is great, and I feel good about the meeting.

My cell phone rings. I look down. It is a little after ten a.m. and it is my parents' number. I don't answer, as I am starting my presentation on our financials. I had spent the last twelve months revising our financial reporting to make the reports actionable.

The number calls again. And then again.

"I am sorry, everyone, my parents are calling. There must be something going on. Give me one second." I step out of our boardroom.

"Juwaa, you need to come right away," says my mom. She is crying hysterically and I can barely understand her.

"Mom, what is wrong?"

"Your dad. He is on the floor. He fell down. He can't get up and is not responding to me. He is burning up." Her voice is shaky.

Before I can respond, she yells, "Please come right away. Now! He is going to die." Her words are quickly burned into my memory.

"OK, I am on my way. I will call 911."

"No! He doesn't want to create a scene."

"Mom, he needs help. I am calling. I will be there in thirty minutes."

"Hurry. I don't know what to do."

I walk back into the boardroom. "I need to go. My dad is sick."

I rush out, leaving my briefcase and computer behind.

What is normally a thirty-minute drive to Frederick I conquer in seventeen minutes. As I drive, the thought crosses my mind that my dad might die.

"Fuck! Rina and now my dad," I say out loud.

I start to cry. "Stop," I tell myself out loud. "He was fine yesterday. What happened?"

I had called 911 and my sisters Linda and Lora. I didn't want to bother Rina, who was undergoing cancer treatment.

When I arrive, the paramedics are loading him up into the ambulance. He is not alert. Linda and mom are crying.

"What is going on? What happened?" I ask the paramedic. "I am his son."

"Well, we believe he had a heart attack, and he is in septic shock. He is running a temperature of 103. We need to get him to the ER right away. Does he have a medical power of attorney?"

Without having time to process what he just said, I answer the question. "He does. I am the agent under his medical power of attorney."

"OK, we need to make a decision. The closest hospital is in Longmont, but we need to get him to Denver. The ER at St. Anthony's is better for his condition."

I respond: "St. Anthony's." It was the first of many decisions I would help make about my father's health and treatment.

Around three p.m., the doctor emerges. He pulls me aside and says, "You are lucky you brought him in when you did. He probably would not have made it. We have a ways to go still. The infection is strong and his body is shutting down."

By six p.m. that night, Dad is stable. They don't rule out a heart attack but determine that he had a major infection from the stents the doctors put in two weeks before. We later learn that this is common in people with bile duct cancer. The cancer doesn't usually kill them. Infections caused by blockage in the bile ducts do, and cancer grows around the stents that are installed to open the duct. The bile enters the blood and strong infections follow. In the months that followed, Dad would have many such infections.

A few days later, Dad is released from the hospital. Unfortunately, we would return often. And one thing became very clear: he would not be able to join us on our trip to Italy the following month.

CHAPTER THIRTY-FOUR

Our Last Day in Cansano

It is our last night in Cansano: June 26, 2013. After the *mercato*, my dad, Donato, and I drive to visit my Zio Pietro at his ranch, which is a few minutes above the town on the way to Campo di Giove. We sample some ricotta, made fresh that morning. So fresh, you could almost taste the grains, flowers, and grass that the sheep had eaten in the pasture the day before. We try some pecorino, which has been aging for six months, and it is nothing like I had ever tasted before. As he cuts it into chunks, I smell nuts. It is grainy, with a soft sand-like texture, and a delicate balance of acidity and sweetness all at once. My uncle pours an Italian liquor for us, and he thanks us for the visit.

"*Mio caro fratello e nipoti, grazie mille per avermi onorato con questa visita,*" my uncle says. "My dear brother and nephews, thank you very much for honoring me with this visit."

The words flow like a river.

The ranch is stunning. A large meadow expands into the horizon. Flowers of every color are in the distance, and the Maiella mountains cast their ever-present shadow. Old farm equipment dots the property.

"Dad, we should buy a place here," says Donato.

"I told your mom that this morning," I respond.

^ ^ ^ ^ ^

The air is cooler today than the day before, and we all walk down to the piazza for the nightly *passeggiata*. Luna joins us, and Aggie, Donato, and Izabella love her. This part of the day has been a highlight to me on this trip. A church bell rings at the top of the hour, which it does all day long. The sound of the bell is comforting. The piazza bursts with people and energy, with today being the final of three straight days of celebrating saints—San Giovanni on the twenty-fourth, San Antonio on the twenty-fifth, and San Nicola on the twenty-sixth. I feel like we have walked back in time to a simpler time.

I reflect on the trip. In four days, I have reached a new level of relaxation and awareness. The Cansano village and Italian lifestyle have deeply moved me in a profound and unexpected way. Only my love for Aggie—love at first sight when our eyes met at *a bar* in Boulder on June 3, 1989—and the birth of our children have touched me quite this way. But this was different. Those events were about my present and future. This trip was about my past and the fabric out of which my parents' lives were woven, as well as the colorful threads out of which they spun the tapestry of our lives. This was about the DNA—not the geeky scientific chromosomes that make up our genes, but the real stuff—stuff that defined, shaped, and formed me, albeit years before my birth. The more you know about your history, the more you know about yourself, I surmise.

I watch my dad. He is doing his thing—chatting with everyone, including visitors from around the world who have arrived the last few days, some of whom he hasn't seen for half a century, not since he was a teenager. There are many hugs, some laughs and some tears. He introduces me to each person and, in each conversation, he makes it about the person he is talking to. He has a way of doing that.

^ ^ ^ ^ ^

It is two years into his cancer diagnosis, and Dante and Donato decide to record their grandfather playing the harmonica on May 5, 2019, which they later released on iTunes. Dad has been very sick, in and out of the hospital. He has lost a lot of weight. He is weak, can no longer drive and, on many days, can't stand for long.

In the middle of the recording session, the home phone rings and my dad answers. It is my parents' friends Sam and Dawn, who are twenty years younger than my parents. The call is on the speaker phone—my parents answered every call on the speaker phone so that they could hear better and both participate in the conversation—and therefore is recorded and on the album. It is my dad on many levels:

Emilio: Hi to both of you.
Sam: We are back from our trip to South Carolina and wanted to see how you are doing.
Emilio: Ah, Sam and Dawn, about the same. I tell you, little by little, it seems to be getting worse. But you know, I am doing pretty fair yet. I got your message, and I think I forgot to call you back. Sorry about that.
Sam: You haven't been back in the hospital, have you?
Emilio: No, no, no.
Sam: That is good.

. . .

Emilio: So, you had a good time on the trip?
Sam: We did. It was very nice, very nice, and we met up with a lot of old friends. It was a good trip all around.
Emilio: Oh, that is nice.

. . .

Sam: Since your grandsons are there, we will let you go. We just wanted to say hello and check in on you.
Emilio: Yeah, yeah. Let's be in touch again. Sometime, if you come around here, if you go to the senior center, call us. If we are home, you can stop by for a little bit.

^ ^ ^ ^ ^

Dad didn't complain. He was not a victim. He turned the conversation back to his friends and focused on what they were experiencing.

He apologized for not returning their call. And he invited them over to visit.

My father.

^ ^ ^ ^ ^

Back in Cansano, I watch my dad talking to his friends in the piazza. He is content. And I am happy that I was able to bring him back home.

That night, we cook many of the items we bought at the *mercato* earlier in the day. My uncle's much younger wife, Rocco's wife and daughters, and Panfilo join us. We have another multicourse feast of grilled lamb, pasta in a light tomato sauce, a salad, sautéed veggies, and fruit.

"I wish you had more time," my uncle says in Italian.

"I know. We will come back soon, I promise," I say in Italian, regretting that I booked so much time on the Amalfi Coast and not as much time here. I didn't know I would have this connection. (We came back the next year and stayed a week. It was still not enough time.)

After dinner, my dad, Donato, Izabella, and I walk to the piazza. It is dark and only a few people are out. My dad is talking to Donato and Izabella, and I walk a few steps behind them. I reflect on the last few days. The soft glow from streetlights bounces off of the cobblestones, which all have so many stories to tell: my parents' innocent childhood before the war; the Nazi occupation and hurried desperation of families forced to leave for the mountains; walking up and down the path after the war to help their families by taking care of their animals and tending their crops; my grandfathers' returning on foot from extended work outside of the town, cutting timber for Rocco and building kilns for Panfilo, with my grandmothers doing everything else to raise their families; my dad walking up the street to buy milk from Mom and, later, to serenade her; and, the townspeople walking down the walkway and showing up when my dad emigrated. These stories show innocence, perseverance, struggle, love, and hope.

Once disconnected stories about my ancestral past, they are no longer.

The next morning, we leave Cansano for Rome and then the Amalfi Coast.

My dad cries as he says goodbye to his brother.

CHAPTER THIRTY-FIVE

Rome and the Art of Negotiation

It is June 27, 2013. We take a train from Sulmona and arrive at Roma Termini, the main train station in the city. The Eternal City is packed with tourists, and it is hot and humid. We pour into two taxis for the short drive to our villa I had rented. As we drive, I am awestruck with the architecture, especially *Monumento Nazionale a Vittorío Emanuele II*, a stunning building made with white marble and adorned with massive columns, monuments, and statues. On the other side of the palace is Basilica San Marco, one of the oldest and most memorable basilicas in Rome. And next to the basilica is the entrance to The Forum. As I watch from the taxi, I am speechless and cannot wait to tour these places that I had only heard of but never before appreciated. It became one of my favorite places to visit in later trips.

Without knowing its history, I rent a villa on *Via Margutta*, a short and narrow street sandwiched between the Spanish Steps and *Piazza del Popolo*.

"Ah, *Via Margutta*," says our tax driver in Italian, after I tell him where we are heading. "One of the most famous and romantic streets in Rome."

"*Veramente*?" I ask. "Really?"

"You don't know?"

"No."

He switches to broken English. "It is filled with beautiful art galleries, restaurants, and people. It was made famous by American movie *Roman Holiday*. Gregory Peck and Audrey Hepburn. You know that movie?"

"No," I respond. How can it be that this Italian taxi driver knows something about American culture and I don't?

"Oh, you must see it. But you can see the street yourself. We have arrived. Enjoy."

The street is alive with a garden-like environment: thick vines growing up the sides of most of the buildings and planters of small green trees and colorful flowers lining the length of the street. In the distance, I see paintings on display outside of shops. Several trees protrude onto the sidewalk, and I see vines climbing up the buildings and others hanging over lights that are strewn across the sidewalk, creating a leafy awning. Only a block off of the busy fashion district in Rome, the street is nearly empty except for people going in and out of art galleries and cafés in the distance. I notice the dark and shiny, almost polished-looking, cobblestones. Different from the decaying cobblestones in Cansano.

We find our building, and I ring the bell on the wall. "Pronto," I hear through the box. Pronto means ready, but it is how Italians answer the phone. I tell the gentleman my name and that we are checking in. A few minutes later, he arrives and takes us up to a stunning two-story villa that overlooks *Via Margutta* below and the rest of Rome from a balcony off the kitchen. The home is dark and filled with art. It is clean but smells old—in a good way. Like your grandmother's home.

"You picked an amazing villa. The story goes that it was once the home to Renato Guttuso, the famous artist. You know his work?"

"No."

"Well, you should. He was one of the most important artists and politicians of his time," says the man in perfect English.

"How did you find this place, Dad?" Izabella asks. "This is cool."

"I don't know. I got lucky I guess."

After unpacking, we walk down the street to find a market. Our plan is to make and cook most of our meals. My dad is quickly drawn to a vendor on the street who is selling the straw fedoras he loves to wear.

"*Quanto*?" he asks the man. "How much?"

The man seems annoyed and says ten euros a fedora, or two for fifteen euros.

"No," my dad says. "I will give you five each. I will buy a lot."

"Mister, this is my price. If you don't like it, go somewhere else," he says in Italian.

My dad turns away without saying anything. "Go to hell then," my dad utters under his breath to himself. He wasn't angry; it was just the way he talked. I had seen this routine before just the day before in Sulmona at the market. Here we go again, I think.

"Dad, if you want them, just buy them. That is not a bad price."

"No. Watch," he says back to me.

"OK, I will give them to you for five," the man yells back at us as we begin to walk away.

"See, that is how you negotiate, Mr. Big Shot lawyer," my dad says to me.

He buys ten fedoras. "Where are you going to put those?" my mom says to him sharply. "We have no room in the luggage."

"Ah, stop yelling at me. I promised my friends I would buy some for them if I saw them."

"We have no room," my mom insists.

"We will make room. And I look good in them," he says with a laugh.

"Your dad, he always wants to look good," Mom laughs.

The routine.

CHAPTER THIRTY-SIX

Cheese in the Pocket

It is a Tuesday night, sometime in September of 2018. It is 2:13 a.m., and the home phone rings.

"Hello," I say, half asleep after struggling to find the phone on my nightstand, first knocking it over. "Not again," I think to myself about the phone ringing.

"Juwaa. I am sorry to call you, but your mom made me call. My temperature is over 101." His normal temperature is around 96 degrees, so this is high.

We are eighteen months into the diagnosis. After a series of infections, some of which were life-threatening, the doctor told us that if he got a high temperature—even a few degrees higher than normal—we should immediately take him in. For some reason, the infections only came in the early morning hours. I had made him and my mom promise to call me if he got a temperature.

"I don't want to bother you, but this damn temperature came back."

"OK, I will be there right away."

"I am sorry."

"Dad, stop. I will be there right away."

I live thirty minutes away. I quickly get dressed and make myself a coffee to go in my Nespresso machine. This has happened half a dozen times in the last eighteen months, and I have a routine: get dressed, brush my teeth, and make coffee. I drive half asleep to my childhood home. I wonder if this is it. Death is not something I had spent much time thinking about prior to 2017. But, with both Dad and Rina suffering from cancer, I think about it often.

I know there is a higher source, and I know there is more to our existence than our human form. But I refuse to believe any one religion is right. How can any one religion be right and billions of people who believe in something else be wrong?

I enter the town of Frederick. My car is the only car on the street.

A year earlier, Dad decided to stop treatment after undergoing one round of chemotherapy and radiation.

"This will kill you faster than the cancer will," he said over and over.

"I don't want to live whatever life I have left sick like that," he told the doctors when they encouraged him to undergo more treatment. He had seen what chemo did to my sister and knew how it made him feel. And the doctors provided no assurances to his or my questions about whether the treatment would cure the cancer.

"Well, on average, patients who undergo this type of treatment live an additional two years. Some go to five years," said one of his doctors.

"But what will his quality of life be?" I asked. "And will it cure his cancer?" I know the answers to both questions but feel compelled to ask. My dad wants hope.

While I respect the work they do immensely, his team of doctors respond in doctor-talk and don't really answer my questions. The doctors repeatedly tell us that the cancer will continue to grow and the infections will get worse.

"They can go to hell with that chemo. Those somana bitches," my dad responded. "When it is my time to go, it is my time."

I enter the house and find him on the floor at the bottom of the steps.

"What happened?"

"He tried to go down the stairs and got tired," my mom says.

"I am fine," he stammers, barely audible.

"Dad, when did you start feeling bad?"

"He started getting sick at around nine p.m.," my mom answers.

"Why didn't you call me earlier?"

My voice and tone are stern, like that of a parent scolding their child. I have now assumed that role with them. Patience, I think to myself.

"We should call the ambulance," I say.

"No, you take me."

"But, Dad . . ."

"No ambulance," he interrupts. His voice is stern.

I struggle to get him to his feet and help him get dressed. We slowly walk to my car, and he almost falls a few times.

We get to the ER at Longmont United Hospital, and they immediately check him in to intensive care. The nurses and doctors know us by now. This infection is worse than the others, and they need to put another stent into his bile duct. They need to transfer him by ambulance the next morning to the UC Health Center, where his primary cancer doctor and oncologist are located.

I have become almost immune to this by now. It is the same each time: We take him in, they get the infection under control with a round of strong antibiotics that cause him horrible mouth rashes, and they either clean out the stent through a painful dental-like cleaning process or add another stent into his bile duct. And the doctors are not treating his cancer. They are treating his symptoms. And each treatment adds new and additional complications.

With each infection the cancer has grown through and around the porous stent. I know he is dying. It is only a matter of time.

Every time, he asks the same question: "Doctor, am I going to get better?" The doctors never answer the question directly. I assume he knows the truth, but he asks each time.

"Can I go back to Italy? I would like to go see my brother."

"We will see, Emilio."

And like every other part of his life, the doctors and nurses become his friends. He shares with each of them many stories about Cansano. Nowadays, he prefers to share the happier memories from Cansano.

"Have you ever been to Italy? It is a beautiful country. The best food, wine. The countryside is beautiful. It is the best country in the world. And Cansano—that is where I am from. Maria, too. We met at age fifteen. I used to serenade her at her balcony."

Dad's charm is still intact, and he captivates them. He invites each of them to his home. "Come over. I will cook for you and we can drink some wine. Not the junk you buy here. The good stuff. The real wine. What do you like to eat?"

This visit is different. After his last infection, the doctors told us they could probably put in only one more stent. That stent was installed today. His medical team requests a family meeting. My mom and I attend with my dad. A group of ten or so medical providers also attend the meeting, including a priest, hospice care providers, and the palliative care group. I have never heard the phrase "palliative care," and the presence of the priest shocks me. I can see my dad's spirits drop. None of his doctors attend. I quickly google "palliative care":

> *Palliative care's main focus is to improve the quality of life for those with chronic illnesses. It is commonly the case that palliative care is provided at the end of life. . . .*

Fuck.

The lead nurse introduces the team, and the palliative care provider talks first. She is sweet and talks in a comforting manner. She has done this before, and my respect for nurses grows. It would grow even more over the coming months, especially for hospice care providers. They are angels.

"Emiliano, what is important to you?"

"Well, my family. Being with my family. Seeing my friends. Playing bocce. Maybe play some cards. Having some wine. Not too much, a glass or two a night. And I have many friends. I want to see them."

He surveys the group. He continues. "I have had a good life. I came to this country with nothing. And me and Maria, we built something for our family. They have opportunities we didn't have." His voice is soft and reflective.

He talks about his journey from Cansano. I tear up but try to hide it. I see a few of the medical providers tear up also.

He stops mid-story. "Am I going to die?" I turn and walk to the window so that he doesn't see me cry.

"Well, we don't like to talk in those words. We are here to help you and help you make decisions to achieve your final objectives."

Final objectives. That phrase resonates.

My dad hears it too. "How much time do I have left?"

"Well, we don't talk in those terms. But we are here to help you be comfortable."

The meeting lasts almost two hours, and each care provider offers some words of encouragement and hope from within his individual discipline. My dad turns to the priest. "I believe in God. I don't believe in everything the Catholic Church does. They do many things wrong. But I believe in God. And I believe in Heaven."

That is my dad. Standing up for his beliefs.

Before the meeting ends, one of his doctors comes in. She pulls me aside and I ask, "Doctor, can you tell me what is going on?"

"Without radiation or chemo, which he doesn't want to do and which we respect, there is not much more we can do. The infections will come back. Stronger each time."

"How much time does he have?"

A few minutes later, I text my sisters and Aggie the response:

> *They just left. 2 hour meeting. Very hard. They were incredibly supportive and nice. Way too much to text and very emotional. . . .*
>
> *The doc later pulled me aside . . . and said a few weeks to a few months . . .*
>
> *I don't know what else to say right now.*

I don't tell my mom or my dad. I don't know what to say.

A few minutes later, they bring Dad some food. He barely eats. As my mom moves the tray, he says to me, "Eat."

"Dad, Aggie is making dinner. I will eat at home."

"Well, take it with you. Don't let it go to waste."

A memory emerges: During our June 2013 trip, we spent five days in a villa in Praiano, with a breathtaking view of the Amalfi coastline. We made regular visits to the local market, buying fresh items for our daily meals. My dad was eating leftover bread, cheese, grapes, and mortadella, while we waited for the private driver I had arranged to take us to the train station on our way back to Rome, the final stop on our 2013 trip.

"We can't let this go to waste. You paid good money for this," he tells me.

"Dad, it is OK."

The driver arrived, and I loaded up the car. The villa was on the cliff, about one hundred stairs up from the road. I lost track of my dad and what he was doing.

We took the car to Naples, and then we boarded a train to Rome. The green *campagna*—or countryside—was slowly rolling by. It had been a long trip, and I was ready to go home. But I was lost in thought as I took in the last few minutes of the beautiful Italian landscape.

"I am hungry," said Donato. He was a seventeen-year-old kid at the time; he was always hungry.

"You want some cheese?" my dad asked.

"What, you have some cheese in your pocket?" Donato said, laughing.

"Yes, I do."

"Ya, right, Grandpa."

My dad reached into his pocket and pulled out something wrapped in a paper sack. He carefully unwrapped it to reveal some cheese we had purchased a few days before in Praiano. He broke the cheese in half and handed it to Donato.

"What? You had cheese in your pocket!" Donato howled in laughter.

"Your grandpa is always prepared," my dad responded, and we all laughed.

CHAPTER THIRTY-SEVEN

The Last Feast of the Seven Fishes

By 2018, Rina's cancer had spread into her lungs, hip, and collarbone. But in August, she is healthy enough to go to Hawaii, her happy place. My sisters, my parents, Aggie and I, and a few of Rina's doctors all chip in to take care of the expenses for the entire trip. She is fighting, trying every chemo treatment the doctors recommend, even trial treatments. And by October, she seems to be doing much better. The treatments make her tired, but the PET scans show no growth of the cancer. This, we learn, is the way to measure success with her disease.

And after being discharged from the hospital in late September, my dad bounces back strongly.

On a Sunday morning in early October the phone rings. I have just returned home from my weekly pickup basketball game. I play twice a week, and it helps keep me in shape. I think I am better than I am, but I am still a decent shooter. Mostly, I love the trash talking. That keeps me young.

"Juwaa," Dad says. "We are playing bocce this morning in Louisville. Do you want to play?"

In years past, I would have said no, I was too busy. Not anymore. Since his diagnosis in 2017, I have been spending more time with him. Some local fishing trips. Visits with him at his home. Short trips to Vail, which reminded him of home. Calling his lifelong friend Concetto Morelli, who lived in Toronto. And playing lots of bocce.

I drive to Memory Square Park. It is a beautiful fall day, not a cloud in the sky, and the temperature in the low 70s. The leaves on the trees are still in their fall glory. Vibrant red, scarlet, burnt orange, and yellow leaves decorate the trees, and some have fallen on the ground around the bocce courts.

My dad has not yet arrived. He insists on driving himself still. This scares my mom, but I know that once we take away his driving, he will lose some of his will to live. Even with cancer, he was the most active octogenarian imaginable. Dad still played cards two to three days a week with his friends in the neighborhood; he loved going to Home Depot for his projects at home, and he went fishing at his club in Louisville with his friend Alberto DeSimone.

He pulls up and parks along the curb. My mom is with him. She refused to let him drive alone. He is in a great mood and full of energy. He is wearing a fedora and layers: a T-shirt, a thick flannel, and a light jacket. He is always cold now. We play two games against his friends Lenny and Paul before Dad gets tired; we win both. As always, he carries our team.

"You guys should just quit now," he teases as we close out the second game. "You can't even beat me when I have cancer." I laugh. Even the bocce players trash talk.

"We are letting you win, Emilio," says Lenny.

"Letting me win, I will show you, young man." Lenny is my age but has become one of my dad's best friends.

My dad tosses the game-winning point. It is a perfect throw and it is clear that the other team is not letting him win. "You still got it, Emilio," says his friend Paul.

"Maybe I am getting better," he says to me.

"I hope so, Dad," I say, knowing better. "I hope so."

^ ^ ^ ^ ^

Within weeks, Dad is back in the hospital, this time with heart issues. Every few weeks, another complication arises, and he spends more and more time at the hospital. There is little the doctors can do. But each weekend, we play bocce, even if only one game. As we say goodbye after one of the games in early November, Dad says, "I love you."

"I love you too." We had just recently started saying this to each other.

^ ^ ^ ^ ^

The Sunday after Thanksgiving, Rina collapses. I rush to the hospital, and the doctor is in the room explaining the test results of the PET scan she had just taken. The tests reveal the cancer has spread to her brain, both lungs, and her neck. The doctors urge her to do intense daily radiation treatments, which she quickly agrees to do.

"Don't tell mom and dad yet. I don't want to worry them," she tells me. "I don't want them to see me like this. Tell them not to come yet."

Some people play the victim. My father raised us not to. A person's character is measured not by how they act in good times, but how they deal with adversity. And Rina is fighting. She doesn't want to die. She is fifty-eight and recently became a grandmother for the first time. And she doesn't want to worry our parents.

As strong as she is, my mom is stronger. Each day, she watches her firstborn and her husband of over sixty years inch closer to death.

I call my parents and tell them Rina is back in the hospital and wants to rest. I don't tell them about the cancer coming back and spreading. They both cry.

"*Mio Dio, che cosa facciamo,*" my mom says. "Dear God, what are we going to do?"

"*La perderemo,*" she continues. "We are going to lose her."

^ ^ ^ ^ ^

It is Christmas Eve 2018, and my entire immediate family goes to my parents' house for our traditional multicourse fish meal. When I was a child, Christmas Eve rotated between our house and my dad's siblings' homes: Uncle Luciano, Uncle Armando, and Aunt Anna, who all lived within a few blocks of one another. Sometimes my mom's family joined us. My family was far from perfect—they were loud, sometimes rude to each other, and always someone wasn't talking to someone else and had to avoid them. But I looked forward to the family gatherings more than anything. I loved the smell and taste of the food. I loved the tradition. I loved being with my cousins. I loved the pizzelle, *cioffe* (fried sweet doughnuts) that my grandmothers made, and the Italian wine cookies that my Aunt Bianca made. I loved the old Italian music in the background. And we all dressed up. I always wore a dress shirt with a clip-on tie.

The tradition was always the same: Dinner started with an Italian bean soup and an olive oil focaccia bread that was like a thick pizza. What followed was a food coma induced by course after course of seafood dishes—fried calamari and fried shrimp with sauteed vegetables; pasta with calamari, crab, and shrimp; mussels; stuffed clams with fried cabbage on the side; *baccalà* (salted cod), anchovies, and sardines, and more vegetable side dishes; grilled eel and sometimes lobster if it was available; and, finally, a salad. And lots of bread and wine. After our dinner, which lasted hours, we opened gifts, with mass from the Vatican playing on the TV in the background. And then we went to midnight mass. Every year. As the families grew, the tradition stopped, and each immediate family had dinner together.

As I drive to Frederick that winter night, I remember those family Christmas Eve events, and a sense of sadness overcomes me. All of my grandparents and several of my aunts and uncles have passed away, and the traditions seem to be dying with them. I never see or talk to my cousins.

Aggie and I take separate cars, as I need to go early to help prepare the dinner. As I enter the town, I go out of my way and turn down Sixth Street and past the home I lived in until I was twelve. My dad built a new home on Second Street that he still lived in. He built many of the homes on that block and owned the vacant lot next to his house that he was saving for one of his kids. "You should build a home here," he told me frequently.

I slow down as I approach my first home, hoping to catch something about my youth. I hadn't lived here in over forty years. I look at our old home and the house across the street where my great-grandmother Anastasia lived. I remember the story of how my dad proposed in the letter to my mom. I think about the other Cansanesi that lived on this block and our frequent visits to their homes when I was a boy. They are all deceased, with the exception of my godfather Carmine DeSantis, and my great-aunt Angela DiGiallonardo. I wish I could go back in time and ask them questions. I would ask them about life during and after the war, about their journey to America. I need to go visit Carmine and Angela, I think to myself. It takes a few minutes to get from Sixth Street to Second Street, and I turn right onto my parents' block.

This will be the last Christmas with Rina and my dad, I think to myself.

The last few years, I have taken over cooking the Christmas Eve dinner. I am not sure how it happened, as I am not a cook. I don't even cook at home—instead, I am Aggie's sous chef. The last few years, my mom and dad made the sauce, but I do most of the rest of the cooking. This year, like in 2017, I do everything, except the sauce, which they still make.

The house is quiet, and I am the first to arrive. "Where is dad?" I ask my mom after arriving and unloading the seafood and gifts. This is unusual. He is usually in the kitchen prepping the food and always greets us at the door. Italian music is typically playing in the background. But there is no music this year. And my dad doesn't greet me.

"He is lying down. Juwaa, he doesn't feel good," she says.

I know this is our last Christmas as the family that I know, and I turn away from my mom to hide a tear. Rina is getting worse, and the words the doctor told me about my dad in September play back in my mind: "He has a few weeks to a few months. . . ."

I put on some Italian music and start prepping the food. I try to bring as much normalcy to the night as possible. Aggie arrives after a few minutes and then the rest of the family starts to arrive. My dad finally comes downstairs. He is in a good mood and says hello to each grandchild.

"You want some help?" he asks me.

"No, Dad, I got it. You should sit down and rest."

Rina arrives a few minutes later. She is wearing a knitted cap to hide her bald head from her treatments. She looks thin and weak. I hadn't seen her in a week and I am, like the rest of the family, startled. She looks like she is dying. The rooms gets quiet.

We have to make this a normal Christmas Eve, I think to myself.

"OK, let's sit down. The bean soup is ready," I announce to everyone. Everyone is uneasy, but the conversation slowly returns.

Midway through dinner, Rina starts to struggle. She is not eating and is having a hard time staying awake at the table. "Rina, you should go downstairs and rest," Aggie tells her.

"Are you sure?" she responds. "I don't want to upset anyone."

"Yes, go," Aggie says. I make eye contact with Linda and Lora as Rina's husband Mark helps her downstairs. We all know that she doesn't have long.

We make it through dinner and everyone moves downstairs to open gifts. This was my dad's favorite part of the night for the last forty years, and having grandchildren allowed him to continue his tradition of making the production out of each gift. And even though all of the grandchildren have grown up, he still tries to make a joking comment about each gift.

At the end of the night, he gives my sisters and me each a card. Inside is a check for ten thousand dollars. This is by far the biggest gift he has ever given. And it means a lot to him. His green eyes are tired, but they are filled with joy. He knows Rina needs the money but tells me that it would not be fair to Linda, Lora, or me if he gave us less.

"Dad, Rina needs the money, and she does not have a lot of time left. Give her the money. We don't need it."

"That is not fair to the rest of you."

He doesn't take my advice.

He starts to talk. "But what I wanted to tell you."

His voice is strong but tender. The room gets quiet. Rina sits in the chair next to him.

CHAPTER THIRTY-EIGHT

Rina's Passing

Death. I don't like that word. It means finality. It conjures up images of darkness and cemeteries with weathered tombstones. It means, for many religions, someone is judging you to decide your eternal fate. Bullshit.

In 2019, I decide *passing on* was a better description. There is more to this life than our time in our human physical bodies. And there is no judgment.

Rina passes on at 2:29 p.m. on February 17, 2019. My dad and I are in the room with her. Her last few days are very hard on her. She is in immense pain and fighting. Her daughter Sarah's birthday is on the sixteenth, and we are all convinced Rina did not want to tie her birthday to her passing. So, she battled. Rina's passing is not like in the movies when you shut your eyes and you pass peacefully. It is a struggle. It is not easy for anyone to witness, especially my parents. No parent should lose a child. It should not work that way. I watch my dad and I wonder if he is imagining his passing. How could he not?

I sit in the corner of the hospice room as family members come in and say goodbye. My children, siblings, nieces and nephews, cousins, aunts and uncles, and some of her friends assemble in the waiting room. It is a big group.

"Live when you are healthy," I think to myself as I watch family members come in crying. Rina didn't have that opportunity. Her life seemed harder than mine. I think about our childhood. When she was seven, she was in a horrendous car accident with my dad, Uncle Luciano, and sister Linda. She was ejected from the car and broke both of her legs in multiple places. She was in the hospital for months and had to learn how to walk all over again. I remember watching her play in a junior high school basketball game a few years later and how she inspired me to play a sport that I would play into my fifties. I remember her buying me my first 501 Levi jeans and my high school letterman jacket in high school. My parents would never spend that much money on a pair of jeans (all I wore before that was Dickies from Kmart) or something silly like a letter jacket. She wanted me to fit in.

I think about us growing apart and a sense of regret overtakes me. Life had happened to both of us and got in the way, and we didn't spend much time together or talk much. I wish I could turn back time and make more.

I look back at my mom and dad.

This is going to be a hard year.

CHAPTER THIRTY-NINE

"Somebody Should Write Our Story"

It is July 6, 2019. My dad has lost over sixty pounds and his clothes hang on him. His face is thin and emaciated. He has lasted six months longer than the doctors said he would. He can no longer drive and has to use a cane or a walker to stand, and a wheelchair. His once thick and strong hands are skeletal.

Over the last few months, we have had many talks about the past and the future. He tells many of the same stories about Cansano and his childhood. He tells me about his struggles in America and the hard work and prejudice he endured. The stories mean more to me now; each time I hear them, I picture the little village, and I think about our walks and conversations over the cobblestone streets.

"Don't do what I did. Don't work like a jackass. Enjoy your life," Dad says.

These words were in stark contrast to what I had heard my whole life.

"I know, Dad. I do."

"You work too hard."

He continues. "Your mom is going to need help. And you have to take care of the real estate and my stocks. I have a lot. You will see."

"Dad, I have it. Don't worry." He has started talking about passing more and more frequently.

Aggie and I pick him and my mom up, and we drive to Vail. He had called me the day before and asked if Vail was still holding its summer farmers' markets.

"Yes, I believe so."

"I really would like to see a market again. Like in Sulmona."

"They have it on Sundays. Let's go up tomorrow, spend the night, and then go to the market."

"*No, non ti preoccupare,*" he says. "No, do not worry."

"Dad, it sounds like fun. I will make reservations at the Arrabelle."

The Arrabelle Resort was his favorite place in Vail. The two buildings that make up the resort are made with stucco, rock, and stone. Each building is designed to look like multiple buildings, with different colors of stucco creating the appearance of different buildings—light blue, cream, olive green, clay red, light orange, yellow, and off-white. Just like in Cansano. Large arches connect the buildings and remind me of the arch that separated *La Partayova* from the newer part of Cansano—the wall that kept the bandits out. The resort resembles many of the ski towns in Abruzzo. Balconies with pots of flowers dot the buildings, and the resort surrounds a cobblestone piazza, which is lined with bottegas, restaurants, and cafés. Terra-cotta pots filled with colorful flowers and a fountain complete the resemblance.

After the two-hour drive, we get to Vail, and he is tired and cold. It is 78 and sunny outside, but he cannot keep himself warm. We check in, and he sits outside on the warm deck of our condo. The deck looks out to Vail Mountain. A large clock on one of the buildings strikes three p.m., and a loud bell plays.

"This reminds me of Cansano," he says. "The mountains look like La Maiella mountains and the bell sounds like the old church bell that goes off every hour in Cansano." He stares into the distance. "I need to go in and rest."

That afternoon, he rests on the couch with the fireplace on. I know this is probably the last time I will see him like this. After witnessing Rina's experience, I am certain it will get worse. Another infection could hit any day. Or his congestive heart failure could lead to a heart attack. The doctors warned of both, and he is too weak to survive either.

Aggie and I make pasta with a lamb Bolognese. We drink some red wine and listen to Italian music. My dad is in a great mood and is feeling better—as good as he can under the circumstances. He doesn't eat much, but he is very talkative. He tells us many stories of his childhood, most of which I have heard. Unlike in years past, I listen and ask many questions. I write some of it down.

"Dad, do you want to go get some gelato?"

"Yes, that sounds good. It is a beautiful night outside."

He is too weak to walk the short distance, so I help him into his wheelchair. "I am sorry to be a burden," he says quietly to me.

"Dad, it is fine."

He is embarrassed with his condition, and I am hurting watching him suffer. I don't have the right words to console him. What do you say? He was always a pillar of strength, and I had spent my entire life trying to please him and live up to his near-impossible standards. Those standards had served me so well and were the foundation for the man I had become. And now, I was seeing him deteriorate, much like the homes in *La Partayova*. There is nothing I can do. He had been there for me in every major event in my life. Even when we didn't talk much in my twenties and thirties, he was the first person I called with major news. He came to watch me in trial and bragged to his friends about my firm and our accomplishments. And I bragged to my friends and business colleagues about his life achievements. "He came here at twenty-one with little more than the shirt on his back, no education, didn't speak English, but yet retired a successful and wealthy man at sixty-two. I can't possibly match that level of success."

The piazza is quiet. Strands of lights create a canopy over a portion of the piazza, and the mountain air brings me back to Cansano for a moment. Dad orders a lemon gelato in a cone, and we sit on a bench across the small piazza. He eats the whole thing, and Aggie and I share a glance. This is the most he has eaten in weeks. We talk for a while before going back upstairs. I don't want the evening to end.

As I help him to his room, he says, "Thank you. This was a nice night."

"Yes, it was."

"Someone should write our story."

"I will, Dad."

CHAPTER FORTY

The Final Negotiation

The farmers' market is packed with people, and I carefully maneuver Dad's wheelchair through and around the crowds of people. We stop at several booths before arriving at the fruit and vegetable stands in the center of Vail Village. One of the booths is selling Colorado peaches and apricots.

"Young man, are the apricots sweet?" asks my dad as we approach the booth.

"Ummm, I guess so," says the pimple-faced teenager.

"Can I taste one?"

"Ummm, no. You have to buy it first."

"How much for a box?"

"A box? Ummm, I dunno. Let me see." He turns to ask another gentleman and says "forty dollars."

"Forty? That is too much. I will give you twenty."

"Ummm, sir, the price is forty."

The boy examines my dad. Maybe he feels sorry for him. Maybe he is charmed by him. After a few seconds, he says, "Let me see what I can do." He turns and talks to the same man, and comes back with, "OK, thirty-six dollars for the box."

"I will give you twenty-three."

This continues for a few minutes. We leave with a box of apricots. Twenty-eight dollars was the final price.

My dad is satisfied. His last negotiation.

^ ^ ^ ^ ^

My father passed away on July 24, 2019. He had been in the hospital since the nineteenth with another infection, but until the twenty-fourth, he was not in much pain. Many family and friends visited with him the last few days, and he laughed and talked about getting out and going fishing, playing cards, and playing bocce. He was his normal charming self.

But he woke the morning of the twenty-fourth in unbearable pain. He had seen what my sister went through and didn't want my mom and the family to go through that again. "I want to go today," he told her.

I arrive at the hospital by nine a.m. and walk into his room. For the first time in this journey, I feel a sense of hopelessness and finality.

"How are you doing?" I know the answer and feel stupid asking the question.

"Juwaa, I am in a lot of pain."

I sit next to him and hold his hand.

"I want to go today."

I don't know how to respond. I had been mentally readying myself for this day, but there is no way you can prepare to lose a parent. I swallow hard and choke back my tears.

He closes his eyes and drifts off, saving me from having to respond.

Over the next several hours, he comes in and out of consciousness. He can barely speak but utters the word *pain*. I ask him if he wants more pain medication, and he slowly nods his head yes. Later, I ask if he wants to listen to Italian music, and he nods his head. I had created a playlist of his favorite Italian songs and put my phone near his bed. He falls back to sleep.

That afternoon, Aggie's Uncle Mike, a Lutheran pastor from Chicago, comes to see him. He had gotten to know him over the years and, like everyone else, considered him a friend. At 3:30 p.m., and surrounded by family, Mike gave my father his last rites. A few minutes later, I asked everyone to leave the room.

I had spent much of my life trying to make him proud and trying to emulate his strength and integrity, not always successfully. After Aggie, he was the first person I called when any event of significance happened in my life. And we had finally reached a great relationship, our own father-son cadence of friendship and mutual love and respect.

I hold his hand. I don't know what I am going to say, but these words come out:

> "Dad, I spent my early years watching and learning from you; my teens and twenties thinking I knew more than you; my thirties and early forties realizing that I didn't know everything I thought I did and learning to be compassionate and forgiving, but too busy to make any time; my late forties and early fifties watching, listening, and learning again, and traveling and laughing together; and now wishing I had more time. I didn't always agree with you, but you inspired and mentored me more than you will ever know. I love you and will miss you. I will never be the man you were."

I leave the room and several other family members say goodbye in private, ending with my mom. She walks out of the room at 4:15 p.m.

My dad passes a few minutes later.

CHAPTER FORTY-ONE

You Can Do It

We are back to Christmas Eve, 2018. My dad is sitting next to Rina and looks around the room. He is surrounded by his entire family. He talks:

"Don't be afraid of anything. Don't tell me you can't do it. That is a bad word."

He pauses, looks around the room, and continues: "If I can do it, if I did it, with zero education in comparison. OK?"

His voice is strong, and he is passionate with his words. He continues:

"I came over here and thank God I grew a great family. Four children, and I have nine grandchildren. Mister young man over here, Dante, we was in dinner one night, on my eightieth birthday. I will never forget it. I will never forget it."

His pace slows down and his voice is now tender:

"As a young man, he got up, he made a little speech. He wrote a beautiful card for the eightieth birthday. And he say, 'Grandpa, we are here today all because of you.'"

He stops and looks around at his family.

"Think about it. You know the meaning? You know the meaning. Here, I grew four children, they are well-educated. I have a son. He is a lawyer. He gives a great, great life to his three children, with a beautiful wife. Which, she do the best for him also. And he tells me all the time."

He pauses and looks around the room at his grandchildren. He continues, but now with emphasis and passion:

"Don't forget my words. Love each other, don't let nobody scare you that you can't do it. ***You can do it***."

My mom then says, "He is not afraid of anything."

He stops and points toward Aggie, Izabella, Dante, and Donato:

"OK. Because we talk about some of those things too, right? You and you, remember? OK, we talk about that. You know, you know what I mean. OK, thank you."

Afterword

On the morning of October 10, 2019, I finish my coffee and biscotti with my Zio Pietro, and I walk my normal path down from Rocco's bed-and-breakfast from *Via Roma* through *Via Oriente* to *Via Due Porte* into *La Partayova*. I stop in front of my dad's childhood home. I walk into the home and am overcome with emotions. I had not yet had the chance to grieve his passing.

Two weeks ago, Aggie suggested, "We need to go to Italy to see your uncle."

It was out of the blue, as we had been planning a trip in late October or early November to Hawaii for her fiftieth birthday. "Are you sure? I thought we were going to Hawaii?"

"We need to go to Italy. We need to go see your uncle. And you need to go. I feel it."

In our prior trips, Zio Pietro was always too busy to be fully present in the moment and spend time with us. My dad was right: Zio Pietro worked too hard. But this trip was different. Maybe he wanted to fill in as the father figure I had lost. Maybe he was finally listening to my father and slowing down a bit. Regardless, on this trip he made time for us and joined us for day trips to our favorite nearby towns. Together, we drank some wine each lunch and dinner. We ate his lamb and ricotta cheese. He showed us his ranch. We talked—a lot—during our morning coffee, walks through the towns, and meals. We laughed. And we cried a bit about my father's passing. I connected with him on a deep level.

Aggie's intuition about needing to go to Cansano that year was right. On December 1, 2019, just six weeks after our trip, my Zio Pietro died unexpectedly after suffering a brain hemorrhage.

As I look around my father's childhood home that October 2019 morning, I feel my father's presence with me.

"Good morning, Dad. I miss you," I say out loud. Not a day has gone by since July 24th that I haven't thought of calling him to talk about stocks, my work, or playing bocce. That feeling continues even to the present day. Over the last few months, I had begun to recognize that he was an important part of every major event in my life and that he took great joy in seeing his children and grandchildren succeed.

Inside his childhood home, I walk to one of the walls and peel off a chunk of the limestone wall that was built over one hundred years ago by my grandmother Filomena's father. I put the piece of wall in my pocket. This tiny village and its people had unlocked a part of me that I didn't know existed, and I wanted a physical part of my dad's history to take back home. A few tears stream down my face.

"Thank you, Dad, for everything you did for us. I promise to honor you each day."

Over the next few mornings, I walk the same cobblestone paths I did with my father in 2013 and 2014. I miss him dearly, and, as they always do along those paths, his stories and our conversations all come rushing back. I say goodbye to him. In a way, I have come full circle. Literally and spiritually.

Inspirations, Acknowledgments, and Gratitude

Writing this book was one of the most challenging experiences of my life. I started writing it on September 6, 2020, in the middle of the COVID-19 pandemic, America's awakening to social injustices and the resulting Black Lives Matter movement, and political unrest and division. As the managing partner of my law firm, I felt a deep amount of responsibility for our employees and clients, and I wanted to help protect them during this unprecedented time period. And I was working harder than ever before, as I was in the middle of my busiest year yet as a lawyer and arbitrator. I was also providing daily crisis management advice to our clients during the pandemic, which was extremely rewarding. Aggie joked that I was "the busiest man alive." But after losing my sister, father, and uncle in 2019, the events of 2020 helped me realize that I needed to focus on something that was missing. I needed to fulfill my promise to my father. What happened next was unexpected. I had never written a book and didn't know how to start. I had no outline. I had a collection of stories, conversations, and memories. I didn't know where the story would take me or, much less, how I would tell it. As it turns out, the writing process was profoundly spiritual and one of the most rewarding experiences of my life. I told my father's story and discovered my own.

I am grateful to so many people who inspired me to write this and who supported me through the process. First and foremost, my wife Aggie, who makes me want to be a better person each day. She sees me and allows me to be me. Her inspiration, guidance, patience, wisdom, love, support, and discernment got me started and kept me going. The credit for this book, our children being good people, and our happy life go to her.

When you are writing a biography in a memoir style, you feel vulnerable, exposed, and doubtful. "Who cares about my story," is a common thought. "Will anyone really want to read it," is another. But my adult children, Dante, Donato, and Izabella, supported me through the process and inspired me to tell the story, as this is their story too. And Dante, thank you for spending the time with your grandfather the last years and documenting so many of his stories. You are like him in many ways. Donato and Dante, thank you for recording and releasing The Harmonica Album. May you make your "milliona dollars" as Grandpa would say. Izabella, don't forget what your grandfather told you.

The team at Radius Book Group was amazing. My publishers Mark Fretz and Evan Phail, first for believing in the project and providing unwavering support for the story and my voice, and then for the incredible steady hands throughout the process. First-time authors need a lot of handholding, and Mark's patience and guidance made the process so easy. A true professional.

My editors Henry Carrigan and Katie Benoit, whose patience with me as a first-time writer and willingness to honor the story and how I was telling it was gratifying and appreciated. Henry challenged me from the beginning, with his first round of edits including a candid comment in the very first sentence of the book that it was cliché, helping me accomplish my objectives for the book. Katie's work was impeccable and extraordinary, taking my raw manuscript and turning it into this book.

Thank you to Pam Marcantonio, who had the unenviable task of editing the Italian portions of the book, which were a combination of proper Italian, Cansanesi Italian, and Frederick Italian, and making it all make sense.

To Jane Friedman and Mark Griffin from Jane Friedman Media, thank you for guiding me through the unknown world of publishing and leading me to the Radius team.

To Jen Huppert who designed the beautiful cover and gave readers a reason to open this book. To Neuwirth & Associates for designing the interior and photo gallery, you set the tone for this classic story.

To MJ Rose, who helped me abandon emotional attachments to my initial working title for the book and for having a vision for how to market this personal story, and then carrying through with that plan.

To Ann-Marie Nieves for helping create a buzz for the book.

To Vic Lombardi, a lifetime friend and fellow first-generation Italian American, who was the person most excited to hear I was embarking on this project and was the first person to read an early version of the manuscript. Vic, you provided me the support I needed to continue the project.

To my sister Linda Gould, sister-in-law Crissy Cardwell, brother-in-law Ron Cardwell, and Aggie's best friend, Heather Kolsch, who read early versions of the book and provided feedback and positive support when I wasn't sure anyone would really want to read this thing I had created.

To my Mom, thank you for being my rock when I was younger and helping fill in many details of the stories in the book.

And finally my Dad, who inspired me to be a better man, from his work ethic, to his unwavering devotion to family, to his love for our ancestral town and culture, to his growth and evolution as a person as he got older, and to the constant reminders to me and my children not to be afraid of anything and that "You can do it." This book is because of, and for, you.

About the Author

Giovanni Ruscitti, Esq. is a first generation Italian-American who grew up in Frederick, Colorado, a small coal mining town that his parents and grandparents immigrated to in the 1950s and early 1960s. A nationally recognized attorney, arbitrator, and mediator, as well as a frequent speaker at national legal events, Giovanni is the Managing Partner of national law firm Berg Hill Greenleaf Ruscitti, LLP. He holds a degree in Economics and an MBA from the University of Colorado, as well as a JD from Denver University. In 2022, he was named as one of the most influential business leaders in Colorado and has served on numerous non-profit boards. He is currently the Chair of the Executive Committee of the Boulder Economic Council, on the Board of Directors of the Boulder Chamber of Commerce, and a member of Metro Denver Economic Development Corp. Board of Governors.

Giovanni and his wife of over thirty years, Aggie Blake-Ruscitti, have three adult children, Dante, Donato, and Izabella. Giovanni and Aggie currently live outside Boulder, Colorado, where they enjoy traveling, biking, hiking, yoga, and Italian wines.